Amazing Stories
to Tell and Retell ▪ 2

Amazing Stories to Tell and Retell ▪ 2

Lynda Berish
Marie-Victorin College

Sandra Thibaudeau
Marie-Victorin College

Houghton Mifflin Company
Boston ▪ New York

Director of ESL Programs: *Susan Maguire*
Senior Associate Editor: *Kathleen Sands Boehmer*
Developmental Editor: *John Chapman*
Editorial Assistant: *Kevin Evans*
Project Editor: *Anne Holm*
Senior Manufacturing Coordinator: *Priscilla J. Abreu*
Marketing Manager: *Patricia Fossi*

Cover design and image: Harold Burch Designs, NYC

Photo credits: p. 6, Photo used with permission from Kraft Foods;
p. 16, Scott Robinson/NYT Permissions; p. 58, AP/Wide World Photos;
p. 65, Corbis-Bettmann; p. 76, Fred R. Conrad/NYT Permissions; p. 80,
Jerry Howard/Stock Boston; p. 94 (left), Tom Walker/Stock Boston,
(right), Index Stock Photography, Inc.; p. 104 (left), Canapress/C. Mikula,
(right), Canapress/Jonathan Hayward; p. 121 (left), Lynn Ball/Ottawa
Citizen, (right), Chris Mikula/Ottawa Citizen; p. 137, Agence France
Presse/Corbis-Bettmann; p. 143 (left), Rollin Riggs/NYT Permissions,
(right), Corbis-Bettmann

Acknowledgments appear on page 171, which constitutes an extension
of the copyright page.

Printed in the U.S.A.

Library of Congress Catalog Card Number: 98-71985

ISBN: 0-395-88441-1

1 2 3 4 5 6 7 8 9–SB–02 01 00 99 98

Contents

121581

www.hmco.com/college

Introduction

Amazing Stories to Tell and Retell 2 is an adult reader for students at the lower intermediate language level. The book is designed to get students reading—and talking! The unusual topics of these human-interest stories capture students' attention and make them want to find out more. The language in the stories has been carefully controlled to allow students to understand the ideas and to enable them to use the stories to improve their reading skills and expand their vocabularies.

Amazing Stories consists of ten units, each of which contains a pair of thematically linked stories. All units follow an identical format. A series of activities before each story is used to pique students' interest and to build background for the reading passage. Follow-up activities after each story help students better understand what they have read and also provide opportunities for vocabulary expansion. The unit wrap-up, called Put It Together, presents a language review and helps students make connections between the stories and the outside world. A key feature of the Put It Together section is the Tell the Stories activity, which guides students as they tell the stories in their own words, first to another student and then to someone outside the class.

THE STORIES

Every story in *Amazing Stories* is true. Over the years, we have collected these unusual anecdotes in magazines and newspapers and used them to motivate our students to read and to discuss what they had read. As we put the book together, we contacted and interviewed as many of the people in the stories as possible to check that the information was accurate and to discover other aspects of the tales that would add spice to these already remarkable stories. We would like to offer our heartfelt thanks to all the people who shared their stories. They were all extremely helpful, and their willingness to have their experiences included in this book will mean a lot to all the students who use it.

THE UNIT FORMAT

Each unit follows a set format.

■ The unit opens with a Let's Get Ready page that stimulates students' interest and gets them involved in the unit. One aim of this section is to explore students' prior knowledge of the topic. New vocabulary is introduced, and students are often asked to make predictions about the readings that follow.

■ Immediately preceding the opening of each story is a Before You Read section, which contains vocabulary work, categorizing activities, and questions relating to the pictures that accompany the story.

■ The Reading Skills section that follows each story comprises many different types of activities. The most commonly used tasks involve general reading comprehension and vocabulary building and reviewing. However, several other types of exercises are featured. Among them are Read for the Main Ideas, Scan for the Details, Use the Context to Find the Meaning, Understand Fact and Opinion, and Understand Main Ideas and Details. Some of these activities incorporate productive language responses in addition to receptive reading skills.

■ The Put It Together section at the end of each unit contains several summary activities covering both stories. Let's Review provides a review of the events and vocabulary in the two stories. Tell the Stories helps students integrate the new language by telling the stories in their own words. They are given a variety of prompts and suggestions to make this process fun and interesting. The Talk About It section provides questions for discussion.

■ Two other features appear in many Put It Together sections. Beyond the Stories contains activities that help students make connections between the stories and their own communities. Writing Option suggests ideas for written follow-ups related to the unit topic.

TELL AND RETELL

One key feature of this book is the way it enables and encourages students to tell and retell the stories. This activity stems from the desire most of us have to share unusual or interesting stories we hear. Students are led through a series of steps that help provide the understanding of the story and the language practice they need to feel confident telling the story.

■ First they read the stories and do the reading and language exercises that accompany them.

■ Next they each tell the story to a peer in class. This provides an opportunity for sheltered practice.

■ Then the student is invited to tell the story to an English speaker outside of class.

These retellings serve two purposes. First, as students talk about what they have read, they integrate the new language and make it their own. Second, the out-of-class retellings provide students who are embarrassed to speak English or who feel they have nothing interesting to say in English an opportunity to feel proud of their ability to tell an unusual or funny story. After practicing the story, students leave the classroom speaking English.

SOME TIPS ON TELLING AND RETELLING

The stories in this book can be used in many different ways. The activities outlined provide a basic framework. The teacher can then build on this framework to meet the needs of students of different ages, interests, and cultural backgrounds.

■ In multilevel classes, teachers may wish to assign the second story in the unit (which is slightly more difficult than the first) to the more able readers. Or teachers may wish to survey the stories with the class and then allow students to select the one they think is best for them.

■ Teachers may assign partners to work on a story together. When they are ready to tell the story to each other, they will be able to help each other remember details and vocabulary and formulate the sentences they need. Contrary to what we may think, students do not get bored telling the same story more than once. They appreciate the chance to practice their new language and build confidence in speaking English.

■ Another classroom activity can involve having each student tell the story to another student who did not read it. During this phase, teachers should encourage the listener to be an *active* listener, asking questions and discussing the story afterward.

■ Another option is to have students tell the story they heard, not the one they read. This encourages active listening and provides additional oral practice.

■ Here are some other possibilities.
  1. Have students record the stories on tape and listen to themselves speak.
  2. Ask students to tell the story to the teacher first and then to another student.
  3. Suggest that students write out the story in their own words before they tell it.

■ After the classwork is finished, the final step is for students to tell the story to someone outside the class. If students have difficulty finding an English speaker to converse with, teachers can help them find ways to structure this activity.
  1. Have students visit another classroom and tell the stories to students there.

2. Arrange lunchtime or after-school activities where English speakers will be present.
3. Have students visit a community center or senior center where they will have a chance to practice speaking English and telling the stories.

RATIONALE

The approach used in *Amazing Stories* is from the communicative model of language learning. It teaches reading strategies through a variety of interactive activities. Students work with partners to reinforce language and to help the other person learn. The dynamic classroom atmosphere that this creates draws students into focusing on content rather than on discrete aspects of language.

Reading skills are supported through a careful progression of activities. Pre-reading activities help students get started. Thematic units help students focus on content. The telling and retelling component gives students a real purpose for reading since they have a specific goal—to tell the story to someone else when they are through. This helps them to read with more interest and to remember more of what they read.

Amazing Stories features accessible vocabulary and simple sentence structures. Fundamental reading strategies, such as skimming to find the main idea and scanning for details, are introduced. The methodology aims to develop students' confidence as readers and to build vocabulary in a supportive environment with the help of interesting exercises and illustrations.

ACKNOWLEDGMENTS

We wish to thank:

- Kathy Sands Boehmer, who encouraged us through the writing stages and gave us valuable feedback about the stories
- Susan Maguire, who suggested these books and inspired us to write them
- Lauren Wilson, who found people and places for us and helped us with permissions
- Kevin Evans, for helping us get the details straight
- John Chapman, whose enthusiasm and skillful editing helped shape the final product
- Allen Dykler, who gave us support and encouragement

We gratefully acknowledge our reviewers for their valuable input and suggestions. Thanks go to the following people:

Jesus Adame, El Paso Community College, Texas
Ann Bliss, University of Colorado, Boulder

Marcia Edward Cassidy, Miami Dade Community College, Florida
Linda Elkins, ELS, Houston
Janet L. Eveler, El Paso Community College, Texas
Rachel Gader, Georgetown University, Washington, D.C.
Grazyna Kenda, State University of New York, Brooklyn, New York
Robin Longshaw
Denise Selleck, City College of San Francisco, California

Special thanks also go to:

- Our loving families, whose patience allowed us to spend many hours at our computers: Johnny, Tara, and Andrea Berish; Charles Gruss, Jean-Baptiste, Gaby, Annabel, Shem, and baby Tasnim
- Millicent Goldman for providing us with a constant supply of newspapers and magazines, where we found many of the stories, and Max Goldman for his keen proofreading

We also gratefully acknowledge the following people, for giving us permission to tell their stories:

- Juliano
- Walter J. Marshall
- Tom Freeman
- Brett Kurzweil
- Julia Somberg
- Tara Berish
- Rob Thompson

This book is dedicated to Barbara Smythe (1919–1989), who always encouraged the love of books and the stories they had to tell.

Lynda Berish
Sandra Thibaudeau

Amazing Stories
to Tell and Retell ■ 2

What's on Our Plates?

Let's Get Ready

Read the list below. Then walk around the classroom. Ask other students about things on the list. When someone answers yes, *write his or her name on the line.*

Find someone who . . .

1. likes to cook _____

2. hates to cook _____

3. likes raw carrots _____

4. likes strawberry Jell-O _____

5. drinks coffee every morning _____

6. doesn't eat meat _____

7. eats dessert often _____

8. eats pizza often _____

9. has a toaster _____

10. cooks rice often _____

Before You Read

A. How do people eat these foods? Work with a partner. Complete the chart. We eat some foods both ways.

	Cooked	Raw (not cooked)
1. pizza	✓	
2. strawberries		
3. rice		
4. carrots		
5. apples		
6. coconut		
7. meat		
8. burritos		
9. beans		

B. Look at the pictures of ways to cook food. Match the pictures to the words.

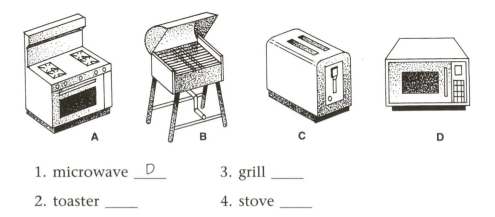

A   B   C   D

1. microwave _D_   3. grill ____

2. toaster ____   4. stove ____

Raw Food

If you go to Juliano's restaurant in San Francisco, you can't get a cup of coffee or a grilled cheese sandwich. All the food in this restaurant is raw—including the pizza, the rice, and the burritos.

Juliano thinks that cooked food makes us sick. "Food is alive, like you and me. When you cook food, you take away some of the vitamins," he says. Juliano never eats food that is over 120°F. His restaurant doesn't have a stove, a grill, a toaster, or a microwave. But he has lots of clever ideas for making raw food taste great.

Instead of heat, Juliano uses water to prepare food. He soaks foods in water to make them soft. For example, he puts beans in water for a few days, and rice in water for two to four weeks. To make pizza, Juliano puts the crust in the sun for 10 hours. This can be difficult in San Francisco, which is often foggy. But Juliano has a friend who lives in a sunny place nearby, so he brings the crust to his friend's house to "bake" in the sun.

Everything at the restaurant is cold, but the pizza and rice taste good. So do the fruit and vegetable juices, made from foods like carrots, apples, and beets. Juliano's restaurant doesn't serve meat, but some people who eat raw food also eat raw meat. Juliano has three friends who ate raw meat. They all got very sick. One of them is still sick.

Juliano eats mostly fruits and vegetables, nuts, rice, and beans. He says he feels very healthy. "Raw food gives you lots of energy," he says. Juliano says he needs only six hours of sleep a night, and he never gets sick.

Reading Skills

Read the sentences. Put a check mark (✓) beside each true sentence. Put an X beside each false sentence. Cross out wrong information and correct it.

1. All the food in Juliano's restaurant is ~~cooked~~. ___X raw___

2. Juliano thinks that cooked food makes us healthy. _____

3. Juliano never eats food that is over 100°F. _____

4. Juliano's restaurant doesn't have a stove or a microwave.

     _____

5. Juliano puts beans in water for a few weeks. _____

6. It takes 10 hours to bake the pizza crust in the sun.

     _____

7. Juliano's restaurant doesn't serve raw meat. _____

8. Some people who ate raw meat got sick. _____

9. Juliano sleeps nine hours every night. _____

10. Juliano sometimes gets sick. _____

SCAN FOR THE DETAILS

Find these things in the story. Write the information on the lines.

1. a drink you can't get at Juliano's restaurant ___coffee___

2. four things people use to cook food _____ _____

     _____ _____

3. something Juliano uses to prepare food _____

4. how Juliano cooks the pizza crust _____

5. two things the restaurant uses to make juice _____

_____

6. what happened when people ate raw meat _____

7. five things Juliano eats _____ _____

_____ _____ _____

8. how many hours Juliano sleeps every night _____

BUILD YOUR VOCABULARY

Which words mean the same as the underlined words? Circle the letter of the correct answer.

1. All the food in the restaurant is <u>raw</u>.

   a. cooked

   b. not cooked

2. His restaurant doesn't have a <u>stove</u>.

   a. a place to keep food cold

   b. a place to cook food

3. When he <u>soaks</u> the food, it becomes soft.

   a. puts something in water

   b. cooks something

4. To make pizza, Juliano puts the <u>crust</u> in the sun for 10 hours.

   a. the top of the pizza

   b. the bottom of the pizza

5. Juliano eats <u>mostly</u> fruits and vegetables.

   a. only

   b. mainly

6. Juliano says he feels very <u>healthy</u>.

   a. good

   b. sick

THE FOOD THAT WIGGLES

Before You Read

A. What do you know about Jell-O? Work with a partner. Read the sentences. Write **T** *for* **true** *or* **F** *for* **false.**

1. Jell-O is easy to make. __T__

2. Jell-O comes in many flavors. _____

3. People first started eating Jell-O 25 years ago. _____

4. You can add fruits or nuts to Jell-O. _____

5. Most Americans eat Jell-O in cubes. _____

6. The man who invented Jell-O became very rich. _____

7. There is a Jell-O museum in New York State. _____

8. Jell-O is the most popular prepared dessert in the world. _____

B. Scan the story to check if your answers are correct. Underline the correct information in the story.

The Food That Wiggles

A. Jell-O® brand gelatin is the all-time favorite American dessert. It's simple to make. Just open a box, add water, and put it in the refrigerator. In a little while, your dessert is ready! Jell-O is fun to eat because it wiggles and it comes in many different flavors, including grape, lime, and raspberry.

B. People first started eating Jell-O in 1897, and today it is more popular than ever. It probably became a favorite food because there are so many different ways to eat it. In the South, people add things such as pecans or coconut to Jell-O and serve it as a salad. In the Midwest, people add nuts, fruits, and berries to Jell-O. Hospitals often serve Jell-O in cubes to people who are sick.

C. Today people buy 414 million packages of Jell-O every year, but when it was first invented, nobody wanted it. It was invented in LeRoy, New York, in 1897 by a young man named Pearle B. Wait. He mixed fruit flavors with gelatin and sold his mixture door to door. His wife called the mixture Jell-O. Unfortunately, nobody bought it, so Wait sold his idea to Frank Woodward for $450. Woodward advertised his new product and gave away thousands of free samples and recipes at fairs, church socials, and picnics. Once people tried Jell-O, they made up their own recipes, and it became very popular.

D. Now there is even a Jell-O museum in LeRoy, New York. People who live near the museum were excited when it opened. They remembered that when they were young, they played in a creek near the Jell-O factory. Every day, the water in the creek was a different color. If the water was yellow, they knew the Jell-O factory was making lemon Jell-O. If the water was red, the factory was making strawberry Jell-O.

E. Jell-O is the most popular prepared dessert in the world. Andrea Cooper, a visitor at the Jell-O museum, said, "I love Jell-O. There are so many ways to prepare it. I always make three boxes at a time!"

Reading Skills

Find each piece of information in the story. Write the letter of the paragraph on the line.

1. information about the Jell-O museum __D__

2. different ways people eat Jell-O ____

3. the history of Jell-O ____

4. how to make Jell-O ____

5. why Andrea Cooper loves Jell-O ____

BUILD YOUR VOCABULARY

Find the word or words in the story that mean the same as the words below. Write the story word or words on each line.

Paragraph A

put water in ___add water___

moves back and forth _____

Paragraph B

square shapes _____

Paragraph C

gave people information about a product _____

directions for making foods _____

Paragraph D

small river _____

Paragraph E

make _____

packages_____

REVIEW THE VOCABULARY

Complete the chart.

	Ways to Serve Jell-O	Things We Add to Jell-O	Color or Flavor
1. in a bowl	✔		
2. lemon			
3. in cubes			
4. coconut			
5. yellow			
6. strawberry			
7. in salads			
8. fruits			
9. lime			
10. raspberry			
11. berries			
12. red			

Put It Together

Make six sentences using the words from Lists A, B, and C.

List A	List B	List C
~~Every year,~~	people add	nuts, fruits, and
People first started	eats food	berries to Jell-O.
Juliano never	Juliano puts the	in the sun for 10
Juliano's restaurant	crust	hours.
In the Midwest,	~~people buy~~	a stove or a grill.
To make pizza,	to eat Jell-O	in 1897.
	doesn't have	~~414 million pack-~~
		~~ages of Jell-O.~~
		that is cooked.

1. Every year, people buy 414 million packages of Jell-O.
2. _____
3. _____
4. _____
5. _____
6. _____

TELL THE STORIES

A. Act out the story "Raw Food" for a small group in the class. Imagine that you are in a restaurant. One person is the customer. The other person is the server. The customer doesn't realize that the restaurant has only raw food.

Customer: Go into the restaurant and order a grilled cheese sandwich and a cup of coffee.

Server: Explain the foods on the menu and how the restaurant prepares them. Explain why you think cooked food is not healthy.

B. Tell the story "The Food That Wiggles" to a partner. Use these questions to help you remember the information, but use your own words to tell the story.

1. What does the food look like?
2. What does the food taste like?
3. How do people make this food?
4. Why do people like this food?
5. When do people eat this food?

Now talk about a favorite food from your culture. Use the same questions to help you. See if your partner can guess your food.

TALK ABOUT IT

Discuss these questions in groups.

1. What is your favorite food?
2. How often do you eat your favorite food?
3. What is your favorite dessert?
4. What kinds of food do you give as gifts?
5. Do you have any special eating habits, such as not eating meat?
6. Are there any foods you don't eat because they are bad for you? Which ones?
7. What do you usually eat for dinner?

SOLVE THE PROBLEM

Discuss these situations in groups. Talk about things to do or say.

1. You're invited to a friend's house for dinner. You don't like some of the things on your plate.
2. A group of friends is going out for dinner. One person is a vegetarian, and another person doesn't like fish. A third person hates tomatoes.
3. You want to invite some students from the class to your home for dinner. The students are all from different cultures, and you don't know what kinds of food they like.

BEYOND THE STORIES

Go to a supermarket or grocery store in your neighborhood. Make a list of the different flavors of Jell-O. In the next class, see which student found the most flavors.

WRITING OPTION

Write about your favorite restaurant or your favorite foods.

UNIT 2

Where Are the Humans?

STORY 1   WHO'S AT THE WHEEL?

STORY 2   ROBOSHOP

Let's Get Ready

A. Match each List A question with a List B answer.

List A

1. What do you use to get money at

   night? __g__

2. Which machines sell food or drinks?

   ____

3. Which machine do you put bread in?

   ____

4. Which machines often build things

   in factories? ____

5. Which stores sell things such as milk or

   bread in the evenings? ____

List B

a. a wheel
b. sunglasses
c. a toaster
d. vending machines
e. robots
f. convenience stores
g. an ATM machine
h. pajamas
i. a mannequin
j. in display cases
k. break in
l. customer

6. What is round? _____

7. What kind of clothes do people wear when they sleep? _____

8. What object wears clothes in a store window? _____

9. What do people wear outside when it is sunny? _____

10. What is another word for *shopper*? _____

11. Where do stores keep expensive things? _____

12. What is another way to say *go in and steal*? _____

B. Discuss these questions in groups.

1. What are some machines people use in public places?

2. What are robots?

3. What kinds of jobs do robots do?

4. How can robots help people in the workplace?

Before You Read

A. Work with a partner. Look at the picture. Talk about what you see.

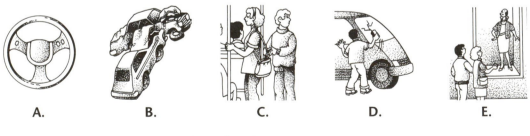

| A. | B. | C. | D. | E. |

B. Match the words to the pictures.

1. a mannequin ___E___

2. a traffic accident _____

3. a break-in _____

4. a steering wheel _____

5. a robbery _____

Who's at the Wheel?

There's a lot of traffic in Chevy Chase Village, Maryland, and some people drive too fast. They step on their brakes and slow down on Newlands Street, though. This is because they see a police car with a police officer inside.

The man in the car is named Officer Springirth. He has worked on this street 24 hours a day, seven days a week, for two-and-a-half years. He doesn't get benefits, and he doesn't get paid overtime. In fact, he doesn't get paid at all. How can Officer Springirth do this? Simple—he isn't a real man. He is a mannequin.

The police force in Chevy Chase Village has 10 people, with 5 cars. Officer Springirth sits in one of the cars. Before Officer Springirth, people broke into 16 cars in two months in Chevy Chase Village. When the police department put Officer Springirth on the street there were no more break-ins in that area. Compared to neighboring villages, the crime rate in Chevy Chase Village is very low.

The most important effect Officer Springirth has is reducing traffic accidents. There is heavy traffic on the busy road to Washington, and a lot of people go above the speed limit. When they see Officer Springirth, they slow down to the speed limit of 30 miles an hour. In Officer Springirth's second year on the job the number of traffic accidents fell from 175 to 157.

People who see Officer Springirth are fooled. He looks exactly like a real police officer, as he sits at the wheel of his car wearing a cap and sunglasses. But people who call him for help are in trouble. Officer Springirth can't help them—he doesn't have any legs.

Reading Skills

READING COMPREHENSION

Read the sentences. Write T *for* true *or* F *for* false. *Correct the wrong information.*

1. People drive too fast on Newlands Street because they see a police car. <u>F   slow down</u>

2. Officer Springirth works five days a week. _____

3. Officer Springirth gets paid overtime for his work. _____

4. Officer Springirth is a mannequin. _____

5. There are more break-ins when Officer Springirth is in his car.

   _____

6. The crime rate in Chevy Chase Village is high. _____

7. There is a lot of traffic on the road to Washington. _____

8. Now there are not as many traffic accidents on the road to

   Washington. _____

9. When people see Officer Springirth, they know he is a man-

   nequin. _____

10. Officer Springirth has no arms. _____

BUILD YOUR VOCABULARY

Read the definitions. Write a word or words from the list on each line.

brakes
neighbor-hood
mannequin
~~**robbery**~~
slow down
cap
police department
break-in

1. taking something from another person ___robbery___

2. drive more slowly _____

3. plastic "person" in a store window _____

4. place where police officers work _____

5. area where people live _____

6. something a police officer wears on his or her head

   _____

7. something you use to stop a car _____

8. robbery from a car or house _____

EXPLAIN WHY

Match each List A action with a List B reason.

List A

1. People slow down __*e*__

2. Officer Springirth can work 24 hours a day ____

3. There were no break-ins in the area ____

4. People who see Officer Springirth are fooled ____

5. Officer Springirth looks like a real police officer ____

6. Officer Springirth can't help anyone ____

List B

a. because he wears a cap and sunglasses.
b. because Officer Springirth was on the street.
c. because he has no legs.
d. because he is not a real man.
e. because they see a police car.
f. because he looks like a real police officer.

Before You Read

A. Work with a partner. Look at the picture. Talk about what you see.

B. Work with a partner. Look at the list of words. Which things can you get from a vending machine in this city? Underline the things you can get.

gum	newspapers	fresh flowers	chocolate bars
coffee	magazines	fruit juice	comic books
sandwiches	a toothbrush	apples	perfume
pajamas	a toaster	a watch	soup
bus tickets	shoes	shampoo	a suitcase

C. Scan the story to find which foods and other items are mentioned. Underline these items in the story. How many are the same as in your city?

RoboShop

It's two o'clock in the morning, and you can't sleep. You want something to eat and a magazine to read. You don't want to talk to a clerk in a convenience store. Where do you go? If you are in Japan, you go to RoboShop. It's in downtown Tokyo, and it's the first store in the world where there are no humans at work. Robots work 24 hours a day serving the customers who come in.

RoboShop is like a giant vending machine. Customers come into the shop and look at the display cases. They write the numbers of the items they want on order cards. Next they punch the numbers into a machine similar to an ATM machine. Then a robot, called Robo, goes to work.

Robo looks like a bucket on wheels. It moves quickly around the store, choosing items and putting them into a shopping basket. Robo always chooses the biggest things first. If you buy a new toaster, Robo will not put it on top of your fresh sushi. Then Robo comes back with your order.

RoboShop sells many things that people buy every day, from food and drinks to household goods, magazines, and cosmetics. It also sells many other things, such as expensive watches and perfumes. In Japan, people buy lots of things from vending machines—pajamas, comic books, even fresh flowers. RoboShop is just like a vending machine but much bigger.

Many people like to shop at RoboShop. "It's fun and interesting to shop here," says Michiko, a regular customer. "The prices are lower because the stores don't have to pay salaries." Other people don't like the idea. Junko, who shops at a convenience store down the street, says, "I don't like it. No one says hello when you come in. People like to talk to other people. You can't talk to a robot."

Reading Skills

SCAN FOR THE INFORMATION

Reread the story quickly to see if the information is correct. Write
T for true or F for false. Correct the wrong information.

1. It is possible to have a store with no human workers. __T__

2. RoboShop is a new kind of American supermarket. _____

3. Customers tell the robot the numbers of the items they
   want. _____

4. Robo moves around the store and picks out the items people
   order. _____

5. Robo puts things into shopping baskets. _____

6. Robo puts the first thing you order into the basket first. _____

7. RoboShop sells only inexpensive things. _____

8. In Japan, you can buy pajamas at a vending machine. _____

9. RoboShop is the same size as a vending machine. _____

10. RoboShop prices are lower because robots aren't paid salaries.

    _____

11. Some shoppers don't like RoboShop because they like to talk
    to a salesclerk. _____

GIVE YOUR OPINION

What are some positive and negative points about vending machines?
Discuss these sentences with a partner. Put a check mark (✓) beside
the positive things and an X beside the negative things.

1. They are open 24 hours a day. __✓__

2. You sometimes need exact change. _____

3. You don't have to stand in a checkout line. ____

4. Sometimes they don't have what you want. ____

5. They are in many different places. ____

6. They are sometimes out of order. ____

7. They never argue with you. ____

8. They are easy to use. ____

9. The food they sell is not always fresh. ____

10. If you have a problem, there is no one to talk to. ____

BUILD YOUR VOCABULARY

Circle the correct word or words to complete each sentence. Use the information from the story to help you.

Roboshop is a new kind of store in (1) New York/(Tokyo). It is a store without (2) human/mechanical workers. It is (3) open/busy 24 hours a day.

Customers look at (4) display/plastic cases. Then they write numbers on (5) paper/cards. Next they punch the (6) cases/numbers into a machine. Robots move around the (7) city/store and put things in (8) paper boxes/shopping baskets. Robo will not put your (9) toaster/bucket on top of your sushi.

RoboShop has a (10) small/big selection of merchandise. Prices are low because the store doesn't pay salaries to (11) customers/employees. Some people don't like RoboShop because they like to (12) talk/listen to other people.

Put It Together

Look at the list of words below. Complete the chart.

	Person	Thing	Activity
1. Officer Springirth		✓	
2. robbing someone			
3. sunglasses			
4. a robot			
5. a vending machine			
6. selling things			
7. a mannequin			
8. a real police officer			
9. a customer			
10. serving customers			
11. an ATM machine			
12. punching numbers			
13. a clerk			
14. a magazine			
15. Michiko			
16. paying salaries			
17. a human			
18. Junko			
19. sushi			
20. a bucket			

TELL THE STORIES

A. Tell the story "Who's at the Wheel?" to another student in the class. Imagine that you live in Chevy Chase Village and Officer Springirth is on your block. Explain what he is and what he does. Explain how you feel about Officer Springirth.

B. Tell the story "RoboShop" to another student in the class. First draw some pictures of Robo. Then draw pictures of the things you can buy at RoboShop. Use your imagination. Use the information from the story, but use your own words to tell the story.

TALK ABOUT IT

Discuss these questions in groups.

1. Do you think using a mannequin is a good way to fight crime?
2. Would you like to have a mannequin like Officer Springirth on your street? Why or why not?
3. Have you ever seen a robot? What did it look like? What did it do?
4. How often do you buy things from vending machines? What kinds of things do you buy?
5. Would you like to shop in a store like RoboShop? Why or why not?

SOLVE THE PROBLEM

Discuss these situations in groups. Talk about things to do or say.

1. You put money in a vending machine to buy a chocolate bar. Nothing comes out.

2. You buy a cup of coffee in a vending machine. The cup doesn't come out, and the coffee spills on the floor.

3. Your school has a cafeteria with hot meals. Now they say they want to close the cafeteria because it costs too much to pay the workers' salaries. They want to put in vending machines instead.

BEYOND THE STORIES

Find a place in your neighborhood that has vending machines. Read the questions below. Write the answers on the lines. Share this information with the class.

1. How many vending machines did you see in one place?

   _____

2. What are two things you can buy to drink? _____

   _____

3. What are three things you can buy to eat?_____

   _____   _____

4. What other things can you buy?_____

   _____   _____   _____

WRITING OPTION

Write a letter to the police department to complain about Officer Springirth. Explain that you asked Officer Springirth for directions, and he didn't answer you.

UNIT 3

Messages of Love

STORY 1   SWEET TALK

STORY 2   I SAW U!

Let's Get Ready

A. Complete the chart.

	Person	Message	Place	Object	Feeling
1. a neighborhood			✓		
2. Kiss me.		✓			
3. I saw you.					
4. happy					
5. a bus stop					
6. excited					
7. Fax me.					
8. love					
9. a flower					
10. candy					

	Person	Message	Place	Object	Feeling
11. Be mine.					
12. shy					
13. a woman					
14. a street					
15. a mysterious man					
16. a coffee shop					
17. E-mail me.					
18. a supermarket					
19. unhappy					
20. a grandchild					
21. Hug me.					
22. a chocolate					
23. a newspaper					
24. like					
25. nervous					

B. Look at the chart on pages 28–29. Which topics do you think are in this unit? Put a check mark (✓) beside these topics.

_____ weddings   _____ finding love   _____ candy with messages

_____ Valentine's Day   _____ eating in restaurants   _____ meeting people in the neighborhood

_____ dating   _____ Mother's Day   _____ falling in love

_____ computers   _____ people in the family   _____ things in the newspaper

Before You Read

Work with a partner. Match each List A item with a List B item.

List A

1. You send this message by computer. __d__

2. What does "date someone" mean? ____

3. What does "Be mine" match? ____

4. You see this kind of message in a

   newspaper. ____

5. What does "engaged" mean? ____

6. You send this message by telephone. ____

List B

a. Page me.

b. I love you.

c. planning
   to marry

d. E-mail me.

e. personal ad

f. go out with a
   person several
   times

Sweet Talk

Valentine's Day is on February 14. It's the day when people talk about love. How do you tell someone you love them? You can send chocolates or flowers. You can write a love letter or buy a Valentine card. Or you can send a sweet message on a candy heart with words such as "Kiss me" and "Be mine."

People started to give candy hearts in 1902. The Necco company in Cambridge, Massachusetts, makes them. It sells 8 billion hearts every year, mostly for Valentine's Day. There are 125 different messages on the hearts. The messages say things such as "Hello" and "Hug me." People have bought the same messages for many years. But now there are some new messages. They say things such as "Page me" and "Fax me."

Who writes the messages on the hearts? Walter J. Marshall. He works for the Necco company that makes the candy hearts. He is 62 years old, and he started to work at the Necco company 40 years ago,

the same year he got married. On Valentine's Day, he gives his wife flowers and candy hearts. His favorite message on a candy heart is "Sweet talk."

Marshall decides what to put on the hearts. "I decide on the message," he says. "But I get ideas from everyone." Last year, he heard his grandchildren say "That's awesome!" a lot, so he decided to put "Awesome" on a candy heart.

Marshall also decides when to take old messages off the hearts, and some people are unhappy about this. They like the old messages, and they don't want modern messages on the hearts. "Don't change any messages on the hearts!" one woman said. "I sent the same messages when I was a little girl." But other people really like the new messages. People who use computers like the messages that say things such as "E-mail me." "I think it's a cute idea," one man said.

Reading Skills

Circle the letter of the correct answer.

1. People give candy hearts
   a. for Valentine's Day.
   b. for birthdays.

2. Every year, the Necco company sells
   a. 8 million hearts.
   b. 8 billion hearts.

3. "Hug me" and "Hello" are
   a. new messages.
   b. old messages.

4. Walter J. Marshall
   a. sends hearts to many people.
   b. writes the messages on the hearts.

5. Marshall
   a. writes all the messages himself.
   b. gets ideas from other people.

6. Marshall got the idea for "Awesome"
   a. from his grandchildren.
   b. from his wife.

7. Some people like the old messages because
   a. the old messages are more interesting.
   b. they sent those messages when they were children.

8. The people who like the new messages are
   a. teenagers.
   b. people who use computers.

REVIEW THE INFORMATION

Match each List A item with a List B item.

List A

1. 1902
2. Fax me.
3. 125
4. Kiss me.
5. 8 billion
6. February 14
7. chocolates or flowers
8. Walter J. Marshall

List B

a. Valentine's Day

b. an old message

c. the year people started giving candy hearts

d. the number of hearts the Necco company sells every year

e. a new message

f. the number of different messages on the hearts

g. writes the messages on the hearts

h. things people send on Valentine's Day

REVIEW THE VOCABULARY

Reread the story. Find the opposites of the words below. Write one word from the list on each line.

unhappy
buy
big
everyone
modern
~~receive~~
small
like
stop
old

1. give _____receive_____

2. new _____

3. big _____

4. little _____

5. happy _____

6. dislike _____

7. start _____

8. sell _____

9. old _____

10. no one _____

Before You Read

Work with a partner. Put the story in order. Write a letter on each line.

A.

B.

C.

D.

E.

1. __C__   4. _____

2. _____   5. _____

3. _____

I Saw U!

A. Ellen is a young woman who was attracted to a man in her neighborhood. She often saw him at the bus stop or at the supermarket. He was tall and dark and had a beautiful smile. Ellen never spoke to him because she was very shy. She didn't know what to say to him.

B. Ellen is lucky because she lives in Seattle. In a Seattle newspaper called *The Stranger*, there is a special section called "I Saw U." It is similar to a personal ads page, where people write in looking for love. But the "I Saw U" section is unique to Seattle. Many people in their 20s and 30s read it. Anyone who finds his or her name in this section feels very excited and tells everyone, "Someone saw me! I've been seen!"

C. *The Stranger* has about 40 "I Saw U" advertisements every week. The section is so popular that people have to wait for months to get their advertisements in the paper. People usually write when they see someone they want to meet in a coffee shop or on the street. People write

things like "Who are you?" and "Would you like to meet?" Sometimes the messages are sad. They say "I wish I knew your name" or "Where are you now?"

D. Finding love is difficult for many people. Ellen, who is 26, is a teacher. She doesn't meet many single men. She thought about the mysterious man for many months. Finally she decided to put an advertisement in the "I Saw U" section. She waited nervously. Then it happened—the young man called her. He said his name was Richard, and he was a computer programmer. He wanted to meet her.

E. Ellen and Richard met in a coffee shop. They talked for a long time, and they liked each other very much. They dated for several months, and now they are engaged. They both say that the "I Saw U" column helped them meet. Ellen says, "I never talk to strangers. I'm so happy I wrote to the 'I Saw U' column. I found Richard."

Reading Skills

Find this information in the story. Write the answer on each line.

1. a newspaper The Stranger _____

2. a city _____

3. a place to buy food _____

4. someone shy _____

5. jobs _____

6. a newspaper column _____

7. readers of the column _____

8. someone tall and dark _____

9. a place to drink coffee _____

10. something popular _____

READ FOR THE MAIN IDEA

What is this story about? Circle the letter of the correct answer.

a. Ellen and Richard's first date

b. an unusual newspaper column

c. a Seattle newspaper

Read the questions. Find the answers in the story, and write the answers on the lines.

1. Give two reasons Ellen didn't talk to the man in her neighborhood. <u>She was shy. She didn't know what to say to him.</u>

2. What is the "I Saw U" column for? _____

   _____

3. What do people say when they see their names in the "I Saw U" column? _____

   _____

4. Why do people have to wait months to put their ads in the column? _____

   _____

5. What are two examples of sad messages?

   _____

   _____

6. Why was finding love difficult for Ellen?

   _____

   _____

7. What happened when Ellen put an ad in the paper?

   _____

8. What are three things that happened after Richard phoned Ellen? _____

   _____

   _____

BUILD YOUR VOCABULARY

Find the word or words in the story that mean the same as the words below. Write the story word or words on each line.

Paragraph A

liked <u>was attracted to</u>

timid _____

Paragraph B

fortunate _____

Paragraph C

ads _____

such as _____

Paragraph D

hard _____

unmarried _____

Paragraph E

went out _____

are planning to marry _____

Put It Together

A. Check your answers to exercise B on page 29. How many of your ideas were correct?

B. Look at these pairs of words from the two stories. Write S *if they mean the same thing. Write* D *if they mean different things.*

1. advertisement   personal ad __S__

2. married   single ____

3. difficult   hard ____

4. column   section ____

5. stranger   friend ____

6. old   modern ____

7. attracted to   interested in ____

8. attractive   beautiful ____

9. shy   lucky ____

10. answer   respond ____

11. in the street   outside ____

12. unique   common ____

TELL THE STORIES

A. Tell the story "Sweet Talk" to a small group of students in the class. Imagine that your friend asks you what to do for Valentine's Day. He or she likes another person and wants to send the person a message.

Explain about the candy hearts. Talk about what they are and why they are better than chocolates or flowers for Valentine's Day.

B. Tell the story "I Saw U" to a small group in the class. Imagine that your friend tells you that he or she is attracted to another student in the school or in the neighborhood but is too shy to talk to that person.

Explain about the "I Saw U" section in the newspaper. Tell the story of Ellen and Richard. Tell your friend why he or she should put an ad in the "I Saw U" section.

TALK ABOUT IT

Discuss these questions in groups.

1. What is a good age to start dating?
2. What is a good way to meet a man or a woman?
3. What are good things to do on dates?
4. How long should a couple date before they get married?
5. Who should call to ask for a date—a man or a woman?
6. What are personal ads? Are they a good way to meet people?
7. Where and how did your parents meet?
8. If you are married or have a boyfriend or girlfriend, how did you meet?

SOLVE THE PROBLEM

Discuss this situation in groups. Talk about things to do or say. You are new to the city or neighborhood, and you are shy. You would like to make friends or find a boyfriend or girlfriend.

WRITING OPTION

Imagine that you see the person of your dreams in a coffee shop or restaurant. Write an ad for "I Saw U." What do you want to say to this person?

UNIT 4

What's That Sound?

STORY 1   MUZAK

STORY 2   TALKING TAXIS

Let's Get Ready

Look at the definitions below. Write three words from the list after each definition on page 43.

actress	restaurant	grocery store	seat belt
passenger	musician	cheerful	nose
famous	chin	relaxed	well-known
~~factory~~	hat	~~business~~	popular
forehead	opera singer	cabdriver	farm
briefcase	annoyed	~~office~~	umbrella

	factory	business	office
1. places to work			
2. entertainers			
3. things in a taxi			
4. places we get food			
5. parts of the body			
6. things we wear or carry			
7. how people feel			
8. words to describe people we all know			

Before You Read

A. Look at the picture. Talk about these questions with a partner. Talk about the answers.

1. Where are the people?
2. What are they listening to?

B. Discuss these questions in groups.

1. How often do you listen to music?
2. What kind of music do you listen to?
3. What are some public places where you hear music (for example, in a restaurant)?
4. How do you feel when you hear music in public places?

Muzak

The next time you go into a bank, a store, or a supermarket, stop and listen. What do you hear? Music is playing in the background. It's similar to the music you listen to, but it's not exactly the same. That's because this music was especially designed to relax you, or to give you extra energy. Sometimes you don't even realize the music is playing, but you react to the music anyway.

Quiet background music used to be called "elevator music" because we often heard it in elevators. But lately we hear it in more and more places, and it has a new name: "Muzak." A company in Seattle makes Muzak for 150,000 locations in 14 different countries. About one-third of the people in America listen to "Muzak" every day. The music plays for 15 minutes at a time, with short pauses in between. It is always more lively between ten and eleven in the morning, and between three and four in the afternoon, when people are more tired. The music gives them extra energy.

If you listen to Muzak carefully, you will probably recognize the names of many of the songs. Some musicians or songwriters don't want their songs to be used as Muzak, but others are happy when their songs are chosen. Why? They get as much as $4 million a year if their songs are used!

Music is often played in public places because it is designed to make people feel less lonely when they are in an airport or a hotel. It has been proven that Muzak does what it is designed to do. Tired office workers suddenly have more energy when they hear the pleasant sounds of Muzak in the background. Factory workers produce 13 percent more, and supermarket shoppers buy 38 percent more groceries when they hear Muzak.

Some people don't like Muzak. They say it's boring to hear the same songs all the time, and they can't stop singing those songs all day. But other people enjoy hearing Muzak in public places. They say it helps them relax and feel calm. One way or another, Muzak affects everyone. Some farmers even say their cows give more milk when they hear Muzak!

Reading Skills

SCAN FOR THE DETAILS

Find this information in the story.

1. three public places where you hear music _____bank_____
   _____ store _____ supermarket _____

2. two names for background music _____
   _____

3. how many people in America listen to Muzak every day
   _____

4. the times of the day when the music is more lively
   _____

   _____

5. how much money musicians can make if their songs are used
   _____

6. why music is often played in public places _____
   _____

7. two places people work harder if they hear music
   _____

8. what supermarket shoppers do when they hear Muzak
   _____

9. what some people say about hearing the same songs all the
   time _____

10. what cows do when they hear Muzak _____
    _____

BUILD YOUR VOCABULARY

Read the definitions below. Write one word from the list after each definition.

lonely

~~quiet~~

relaxed

enjoy

boring

locations

recognize

songwriter

1. the opposite of loud _____quiet_____

2. a word that means "places" _____

3. a person who writes songs _____

4. a word that means "know something that you see or hear"

   _____

5. a word that means "feel alone" _____

6. the opposite of "nervous" _____

7. a word that means "not interesting" _____

8. a word that means "to like" _____

GIVE YOUR OPINION

Talk about these sentences in groups. Say if you agree or disagree with each sentence. Explain why.

1. I like to listen to music when I wait in a bank or restaurant.

2. The music we hear in public is usually boring.

3. People who listen to music at work are more relaxed.

4. I don't like to hear music everywhere I go.

5. When I hear music in a store or bank, I sing the same song all day.

6. I like to listen to music when I read or study.

7. Quiet music is OK in a store or restaurant, but I don't like loud music.

8. I like to sing along to the songs I hear.

Before You Read

A. Work with a partner. Look at the picture. Talk about what you see.

B. Work with a partner. Read each question, and circle the letter of the correct answer.

1. What is New York City like?

   a. noisy   b. small   c. quiet

2. How is noise level measured?

   a. in kilowatts   b. in liters   c. in decibels

3. How many taxis are in New York City?

   a. 2,000   b. 6,000   c. 12,000

4. Why are many people injured in New York taxis?

   a. The taxis are old.

   b. They don't wear seat belts.

   c. Taxi drivers can't find the streets.

C. Scan the story to check your answers to the questions. Underline the information in the story.

Talking Taxis

Many people think New York is a noisy city. In fact, scientists who study noise say that the average noise level in New York is 72.5 decibels. This is a little louder than normal conversation, which is 65 decibels. The noise level comes from having so many people and cars in the same area.

Now even the insides of taxis are noisy. When you get into a taxi, you hear the voice of a well-known opera singer, sports announcer, or Broadway actress giving instructions. That's right. The voice of a famous person tells you what to do. One popular singer gives this message: "Cats have nine lives, but you have only one, so buckle your seat belt!" Other voices say things such as "Don't forget to collect all your belongings." (People often leave hats, umbrellas, and briefcases in taxis.)

There is a good reason for the messages. There are more than 12,000 cabs in New York, and every year taxis get into more than 15,000 accidents. In an accident, people who don't wear seat belts hit the partition in the taxi. They can bruise their foreheads or break their noses or chins. Every year, about 11,000 people are injured in this way.

Many people are annoyed by the voices. Cabdrivers in particular dislike the messages. "I play the messages 12 hours a day. I hear the same voices 60 times a day. It makes me crazy," says Amir, a 45-year-old cabdriver. "But if I don't play the messages, I get fined $100." A lot of passengers complain, too. "It's too much noise," says a passenger. "I asked the driver to turn off the message, but he said he can't."

Other people think the voices are a great idea. One taxi driver says, "People like to hear the famous voices, and they put on their seat belts more often." And passengers from out of town really like the idea. "Most of the time, taxi drivers are in a bad mood," says Melanie Benton, who visits New York often on business. "It's nice to hear a cheerful voice when you get into a cab."

Reading Skills

Match each List A item with a List B item.

List A

1. the number of times Amir hears the message daily _____60_____

2. the level of normal conversation

   _____

3. the number of people injured in taxis

   each year _____

4. Amir's age _____

5. the fine for not playing messages

   _____

6. the number of taxis in New York City

   _____

7. the noise level in New York City

   _____

8. the number of hours Amir hears the messages

   every day _____

9. the number of taxi accidents every year

   _____

List B

65 decibels
12,000
$100
45 years old
72.5 decibels
12
11,000
~~60~~
15,000

Complete each sentence with information from the text.

1. Scientists who study noise **say that** the noise level in New York
   is 72.5 decibels
   _____.

2. Famous voices tell you what to do **when** _____
   _____.

3. Taxi passengers are injured **when** _____
   _____.

4. Cabdrivers dislike the messages **because** _____
   _____.

5. **If** drivers don't play the messages, _____
   _____.

6. Passengers complain about the messages **because** _____
   _____.

7. **When** people hear famous voices, _____
   _____.

8. Melanie Benton likes the messages **because she likes to** _____
   _____.

BUILD YOUR VOCABULARY

Match each List A item with a List B item.

List A

1. put on a seat belt __g__

2. noise level ____

3. give instructions ____

4. belongings ____

5. cabs ____

6. noisy ____

7. get hurt ____

8. dislike ____

9. famous ____

10. town ____

11. in particular ____

12. remember ____

List B

a. taxis

b. tell you what to do

c. hats, umbrellas, briefcases

d. don't forget

e. be annoyed by

f. especially

g. buckle up

h. loud

i. decibels

j. well-known

k. city

l. be injured

Put It Together

Make six sentences using the words from Lists A, B, and C.

List A	List B	List C
~~Many people~~	often belong to	in taxis.
A company in Seattle	there are 15,000 accidents	when their songs are used.
Some famous songwriters	hear the same messages	for 150,000 locations.
Taxi drivers	are happy	60 times a day.
Every year,	makes Muzak	~~when they listen to music.~~
Voices in taxis	~~feel relaxed~~	famous people.

1. Many people feel relaxed when they listen to music.
2. _____
3. _____
4. _____
5. _____
6. _____

TELL THE STORIES

Tell the two stories in this unit. To practice, tell the stories to another student in the class. Then tell the two stories to a friend or someone in your family after class.

After you tell the stories to another person, ask him or her these questions. Share this information with the class.

1. Where do you hear Muzak?
2. Do you like to hear Muzak? Why or why not?
3. Do you think that talking taxis are a good idea? Why or why not?

TALK ABOUT IT

Discuss these questions in groups.

1. Do you like music?
2. What is your favorite kind of music?
3. Do you like to hear music in public places? Why or why not?
4. Do you like to hear music when you wait on hold on the telephone? Why or why not?

SOLVE THE PROBLEM

Discuss these situations in groups. Talk about things to do or say.

1. You go into a restaurant for a quiet dinner. The music is so loud you can't have a conversation with your friend.

2. You get into a taxi and discover that the seat belts are broken and the taxi is dirty.

3. It is midnight, and your neighbors are playing loud music. You have to get up early the next morning, and you need your sleep.

4. You are in a taxi. The taxi driver is very rude and is driving fast. You feel uncomfortable.

BEYOND THE STORIES

Work with a partner. After class, go to a bank, some stores, or other public places. Answer these questions. Share this information with the class.

1. In which places do you hear Muzak?

2. Which songs do you hear?

3. How do you feel about the music in these places?

WRITING OPTION

A. Write a letter to a restaurant or bank. Explain what you think of the Muzak.

B. Write a letter to the taxi company in New York. Explain what you think of talking taxis.

Working Up High

Let's Get Ready

A. Interview three students. Find three jobs that people in their families do. Write the jobs in the chart.

Name of Student			
1.			
2.			
3.			

B. Work in groups. Discuss this list of jobs. What does each person do?

flight attendant   courier   police officer

ambulance driver   flagpole painter   firefighter

window washer   letter carrier

C. Discuss the meaning of the words dangerous, interesting, and useful. Then complete the chart with your group using the jobs listed above. List the jobs from most (number 1) to least (number 8) in each category.

	Dangerous	Interesting	Useful
1.			
2.			
3.			
4.			
5.			
6.			
7.			
8.			

D. Compare your lists with lists from other groups. Explain why you chose the order you did.

Before You Read

A. Work with a partner. Look at the picture. Talk about what you see.

B. Discuss these questions in groups.

1. Are you afraid of heights?
2. What are some jobs that people do in the air?
3. How dangerous are these jobs?
4. Would you like to do a job that is high up? Why or why not?

At the Top of the World

A. Tom Freeman sees the United States differently than most of us see it. He looks down at the world from the air. Tom has an unusual job: painting flagpoles. The flagpoles can be 50 to 80 feet tall. Some poles are very narrow. They may be six inches wide at the bottom and only one inch wide at the top.

B. Tom is 54 years old. He started painting flagpoles 10 years ago when a friend asked him for help painting a flagpole. Tom liked the work and bought the equipment he needed to paint more. "I got my first job painting a flagpole at the University of Pennsylvania, and I've been painting flagpoles ever since," he says. Now Tom advertises his services to colleges, schools, communities, and post offices. "I have a unique business, so it's important to tell people what I do," he says.

C. Tom travels all over the United States to paint flagpoles. He paints about 150 to 200 poles a year. He usually starts in April and works until October or November, when the weather gets cold. Sometimes he works in California or Texas in the winter.

D. What is the hardest thing about painting flagpoles? "You climb a big pole, and you hope it doesn't break," Tom says. "This job looks pretty scary from the ground, and it can be dangerous. You have to climb up really high." Some poles are very old. They are rusty, and they are difficult to paint. They can also be cracked. "I always hope they don't break when I'm painting them," Tom says.

E. The tallest pole Tom ever painted was 137 feet high. But he will always remember a pole he painted in Kansas. "It was 30 feet high, and the wind bent it over. I landed in a football field." Tom went to the hospital because he was bruised and sore. Fortunately, he didn't break any bones, and he was soon back at work.

Reading Skills

Complete the sentences with information from the story. Write the information on the lines.

1. Tom Freeman looks down on the world **because** _he paints_
   _flagpoles_____.

2. Tom started painting flagpoles **when** _____
   _____.

3. Tom liked the work, **so** _____
   _____.

4. He says it's important to tell people about his work **because**
   _____.

5. Tom travels across the country **in order to** _____
   _____.

6. Tom stops painting in November **because** _____
   _____.

7. Painting flagpoles can be dangerous **because** _____
   _____.

8. The poles are difficult to paint **because** _____
   _____.

9. Tom will remember the 30-foot flagpole in Kansas **because**
   _____.

10. He went to the hospital **because** _____
    _____.

Reread the story. Read the questions below. Write the correct answer on each line.

1. Which part of a flagpole is the widest—the top, the middle, or the bottom? _the bottom_

2. How old was Tom when he started painting flagpoles?

   _____

3. In which places does Tom advertise his services?

   _____

4. How many flagpoles does Tom paint each year? _____

5. How many months a year does Tom paint flagpoles?

   _____

6. What was 137 feet high? _____

7. What was 30 feet high? _____

BUILD YOUR VOCABULARY

Find the word or words in the story that mean the same as the words below. Write the story word or words on each line.

Paragraph A

special or different ___unusual___

thin _____

Paragraph B

began _____

tools or supplies _____

there is only one like it _____

Paragraph C

goes _____

becomes _____

Paragraph D

most difficult _____

go up _____

broken _____

Paragraph E

highest _____

hurt _____

CLASSIFY THE EXAMPLES

Find examples in List B that match the general categories in List A.

List A

1. injuries __c__

2. states in the United States ____

3. places that have flagpoles ____

4. activities ____

5. descriptions of flagpoles ____

6. months of the year ____

7. problems with some

   flagpoles ____

List B

a. travel, paint, climb

b. narrow, tall

c. bruised, sore, broken bones

d. California, Texas

e. colleges, schools,
   post offices

f. April, October, November

g. rusty, cracked, old

Before You Read

A. Work with a partner. Look at the picture on page 65. Talk about what you see.

B. What do you know about air travel? Work with a partner. Read the sentences. Write **T** *for* **true** *and* **F** *for* **false.**

1. People started to travel by plane in the 1920s. ___T___

2. Both male and female flight attendants work on airplanes today. _____

3. People often got sick in early airplanes. _____

4. Stewardesses were women who worked on airplanes. _____

5. The first airplanes were very cold. _____

6. You could open the windows on the first airplanes. _____

7. Only men worked on the first airplanes. _____

8. The first airplanes were very quiet. _____

9. It wasn't expensive to travel by air in the 1920s. _____

10. People were served meals on the first airplanes. _____

C. Scan the story to check your answers to the questions.

Flying the Skies

A. Today air travel is very common, but the first flights were very different from today.

B. When air travel began in the 1920s it was very expensive, and most people continued to travel by train or ship. Only the rich and adventurous could afford to fly, and they expected the same kind of luxury they could get on a ship. The first airplanes had chairs with cushions, and tables set with linen tablecloths, china, cutlery, and fresh flowers. The passengers ate wonderful meals, served by men wearing white jackets and gloves. At night, they slept on foldout beds, with sheets, pillows, and blankets. In the morning, the servers, called stewards, brought the passengers tea in china cups.

C. Unfortunately, the trip wasn't always smooth. The first planes shook, and many passengers became sick. The vibrations also caused many dishes to fall and break. Passengers were able to open the windows to get fresh air, but when they landed mud came in the window. The planes were freezing, so people had to bundle up in warm coats, scarves, and gloves. The planes were also extremely noisy, so people couldn't talk to each other. To communicate, they had to yell or write notes.

D. Back then only men worked as flight attendants. Their job was to carry passengers' luggage, serve the meals, and keep people safe and warm. They even put cotton in passengers' ears to block the noise, and gave them brown paper bags when they felt sick.

E. In the 1930s, women began to work on airplanes. The first female flight attendants were all registered nurses. They wore green suits on the ground, but in the air they wore white nurses uniforms with caps. During the flight they held the hands of scared passengers, and helped passengers who became sick. After the flight, they had to dust the plane inside and out, and help the pilot put in fuel.

F. Gradually, more women were hired. They were called "stewardesses." Only young and attractive women were accepted, and the airlines told them to smile at the passengers all the time. Stewardesses were not allowed to marry or have children.

G. Today both men and women work as flight attendants. They wear the same kinds of uniforms, and do the same kind of work.

Reading Skills

UNDERSTAND THE DETAILS

Some information in each sentence incorrect. Cross it out, and write the correct information on the line.

1. People began to travel by plane in the ~~1950s~~. _____1920s_____

2. Everyone could afford to fly in the 1920s. _____

   _____

3. The first planes were very smooth, and many passengers

   became sick. _____

4. When the planes landed, water came in the windows.

   _____

5. The planes were very quiet, so people had to yell. _____

   _____

6. At first, only women could become flight attendants.

   _____

7. Women wore green suits in the air in the 1930s. _____

_____

8. After the flight, the passengers helped the pilot put in fuel.

_____

9. The airlines told stewardesses to laugh at the passengers

all the time. _____

10. Stewardesses could not divorce or have children. _____

_____

REVIEW THE VOCABULARY

Cross out the word in each group that doesn't belong.

1. sheets   blankets   ~~suits~~   pillows

2. expensive   night   rich   luxury

3. coats   scarves   passengers   gloves

4. cup   suit   cap   uniform

5. stewardess   flight attendant   steward   meals

6. cutlery   dishes   cups   mud

7. chairs   tea   beds   tables

When did each thing happen? Complete the chart.

	In the 1920s	In the 1930s	Now
1. Women began to work as flight attendants.		✓	
2. Both men and women are flight attendants.			
3. Flight attendants couldn't marry or have children.			
4. Passengers needed warm clothes.			
5. Passengers slept with sheets and blankets.			
6. People could open the windows on airplanes.			
7. Flight attendants were registered nurses.			
8. Flight attendants helped the pilot put fuel in the plane.			
9. Men and women wear the same kinds of uniforms.			
10. Mud came in the windows.			
11. Airlines told flight attendants to smile all the time.			
12. Passengers ate at tables with linen tablecloths.			

BUILD YOUR VOCABULARY

Find the word or words in the story that mean the same as the words below. Write the story word or words on each line.

Paragraph A

have a lot of money _____rich_____

Paragraph B

pillows _____

spoons, forks, and knives _____

Paragraph C

went to the ground _____

wet dirt _____

talk very loud _____

Paragraph D

suitcases _____

stop _____

Paragraph E

hats _____

clean _____

Paragraph F

after a while _____

pretty _____

Paragraph G

clothes people wear for a job _____

Put It Together

Use the words below to complete the crossword puzzle. Read the stories again to help you.

Across

services

flight attendants

~~passengers~~

noisy

uniforms

steward-esses

air

modern

tallest

Airplanes

high

safe

sick

break

1. People who travel on airplanes are called __passengers__ .

5. When you travel by air, _____ _____ serve food and drinks and talk about safety.

7. Long ago, people didn't travel by _____ the way we do today.

9. Special clothes that people wear for their jobs are called

_____ .

11. Business people have to advertise their _____ to get customers.

13. The first airplanes were cold and noisy, but _____ airplanes are more comfortable.

14. The _____ pole Tom painted was 137 feet high.

Down

2. Flight attendants make sure that passengers are _____ .

3. When Tom Freeman paints a flagpole, he worries that it can

_____ .

4. In the 1930s, flight attendants were called _____ .

6. Early airplanes were so _____ that people had to yell or write notes.

8. _____ are much faster than cars, and they travel in the air.

10. Tom Freeman has to climb very _____ to repair flagpoles.

12. Early airplane travelers often became _____ when the plane shook.

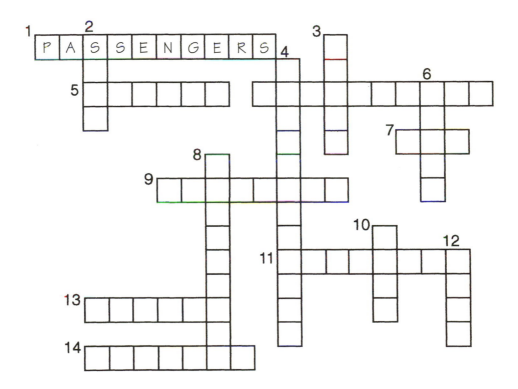

TELL THE STORIES

A. Tell the story "At the Top of the World" to a small group of students in the class. Imagine that you are Tom Freeman. Use the information from the story, but add your own ideas as well. Talk about these things.

1. how you started doing this job
2. what you like about the job
3. what you dislike about the job
4. how dangerous the job can be
5. your most interesting experience

B. Tell the story "Flying the Skies." To practice, tell the story to another student in the class. Then tell the story to a friend or someone in your family after class.

After you tell the story to another person, ask him or her these questions. Write the answer on each line. Share this information with the class.

1. Do you like to fly? _____

2. What do you like most about air travel? _____

3. What do you like least about air travel? _____

4. When was the last time you traveled by airplane?

   _____

5. Where did you go? _____

6. How long did it take? _____

7. What did the flight attendants wear? _____

8. What kind of food did the flight attendants serve?

   _____

9. What information did the flight attendants give you?

   _____

TALK ABOUT IT

Discuss these questions in groups.

1. Do you know anyone who has a special fear or phobia, such as a fear of high places?
2. How do you feel about being in high places? Is being up in an airplane the same as being in a tall building?
3. Are there any high places where you would not want to go?
4. What can a person who is afraid of heights do if he or she has to go up in a tall building?

SOLVE THE PROBLEM

Discuss these situations in groups. Talk about things to do or say.

1. A younger person in your family wants to become a flight attendant.
2. A younger person in your family wants to do a dangerous job, such as painting flagpoles.
3. Your friend asks you to go mountain climbing. You are afraid of heights.
4. You are selected to go on a trip into outer space.

WRITING OPTION

Select one of the jobs in this unit—flight attendant or flagpole painter. Tell what some of the good things and bad things about the job are.

UNIT 6

What Makes You Hungry?

STORY 1   GOOD ENOUGH TO EAT

STORY 2   EAT CHOCOLATE: IT'S GOOD FOR YOU!

Let's Get Ready

A. Read the list below. Then walk around the classroom. Ask other students about things on the list. When someone answers yes, *write his or her name on the line.*

Find someone who...

1. loves chocolate _____

2. eats corn flakes and milk _____

3. can make tomato sauce _____

4. prefers dark chocolate to milk chocolate _____

5. uses recipes from magazines or newspapers _____

6. uses food coupons at the grocery store _____

7. doesn't like chocolate _____

8. likes to drink chocolate milk _____

9. likes garlic _____

10. feels guilty when he or she eats chocolate _____

B. Find the opposite of each word in the list.

sweet

thin

asleep

easy

smooth

solid

illness

dark
chocolate

stale

~~crisp~~

full

guilt

1. soggy _____ *crisp* _____

2. milk chocolate _____

3. pleasure _____

4. alert _____

5. hungry _____

6. difficult _____

7. health _____

8. bitter _____

9. fresh _____

10. liquid _____

11. fuzzy _____

12. thick _____

Before You Read

Match the definitions with the people or things they define.

1. a person who prepares food for advertising _c_

2. a storekeeper who sells food ____

3. words and pictures used to sell something ____

4. a piece of paper that offers a price discount ____

5. things people buy ____

6. a photography session ____

a. products
b. a grocer
c. a food stylist
d. a photo shoot
e. an advertisement
f. a food coupon

Good Enough to Eat

A. Think about the pictures of food you see in magazines. The turkey looks tender and juicy. The soup looks hot and thick. The ice cream looks rich and creamy, and the pudding looks velvety smooth. Don't you get hungry just looking at them? Be careful though. Not everything is the way it looks.

B. Brett Kurzweil knows that. He works as a food stylist in New York City, and his job is preparing food for advertisements. Food ads cost thousands of dollars. A single food coupon can reach 30 million people, so advertisers want their products to look good. Brett Kurzweil's challenge is to do that under difficult circumstances.

C. At a photo session, food can sit for hours under hot lights. Brett has to use his imagination to come up with techniques to keep the food looking delicious and natural. For example, because corn flakes get soggy in milk, Brett sprays hair tonic on the corn flakes. That way the corn flakes can sit for hours and still look crisp. He also uses instant mashed potatoes to fill in fruit pies. And to make roasted garlic heads look fresh, he uses a small paintbrush

to coat them with liquid soap. Other tools of the trade include glue and pins, to keep foods from separating.

D. Brett says, "I start with the best-looking food I can find." Once he needed fresh garlic for a tomato sauce ad. He visited six different stores looking for several perfect garlic heads of uniform size. He bought 117 heads of garlic and picked out 34 of the best garlic heads to roast. "Grocers who see me picking through their pyramids of foods hate me," Brett confesses. Another time he needed 10 cakes for an advertisement. He had to bake 80 cakes to get 10 perfect ones.

E. Sometimes the biggest challenge is to find the right fruits and vegetables. "Finding pumpkins in June or cherries in December isn't always easy," Brett says. "Once I had a real problem. I needed peaches for an ad, but it was too early in the season, and I couldn't find any." Suddenly an idea came to Brett as he was walking past a pharmacy. "I used foot spray to give nectarines a fuzzy look. It worked fine—as long as no one looked too closely," he says.

Reading Skills

SKIM FOR THE INFORMATION

*Skim the story to check the information below. Write **T** for **true** or **F** for **false** after each statement. Correct the wrong information.*

1. Brett Kurzweil's job is photographing food for advertisements.

   F   preparing food

2. The food in photographs looks good because it's natural. _____

3. Brett uses hair tonic on corn flakes to preserve their color. _____

4. Food stylists like Brett are popular with grocers. _____

5. The food Brett uses must be perfect. _____

6. Brett can always find the food he needs easily. _____

SCAN FOR THE DETAILS

Write the details from the story on the lines.

1. a kind of meat _____turkey_____

2. a food that looks rich and creamy _____

3. Brett's job _____

4. the number of people a food coupon can reach _____

5. what Brett uses to fill in fruit pies _____

6. three tools Brett uses to keep food looking good _____

   _____ _____

7. the number of heads of garlic he once bought _____

8. the number of perfect cakes he needed _____

9. the fruit Brett was looking for _____

10. what Brett used to give nectarines a fuzzy look _____

USE THE CONTEXT TO FIND THE MEANING

Sometimes pronouns and other words are used to hold a story together. It is important to know exactly what these words refer to. Use the context to find the meaning of the underlined words below. Then write the words or ideas they refer to on the lines.

1. Paragraph A: looking at <u>them</u> *pictures of food in magazines*

2. Paragraph B: knows <u>that</u> _____

3. Paragraph B: challenge is to do <u>that</u> _____

4. Paragraph C: to coat <u>them</u> _____

5. Paragraph D: ten perfect <u>ones</u> _____

6. Paragraph E: I couldn't find <u>any</u> _____

RECYCLE THE VOCABULARY

Match the words from the story that go together.

1. photo *e*

2. roasted _____

3. liquid _____

4. tomato _____

5. foot _____

6. magazine _____

7. mashed _____

8. food _____

a. stylist
b. soap
c. garlic
d. ads
e. shoot
f. potatoes
g. sauce
h. spray

Before You Read

A. What do you know about chocolate? Work with a partner.
Read the questions and answer **T** *for* **true** *or* **F** *for* **false**.

1. Most of the chocolate we buy is high in fat and sugar. __T__

2. Thanksgiving is a holiday that is associated with chocolate. ____

3. People first used chocolate as a drink. ____

4. The first chocolate people ate was very bitter. ____

5. Most Americans prefer dark chocolate to milk chocolate. ____

6. Chocolate has a variety of vitamins and minerals. ____

7. Chocolate has a chemical that makes us feel guilty. ____

8. Good-quality chocolate is low in fat and sugar. ____

B. Scan the story to check your answers to the questions above.
Correct the information that is wrong.

Eat Chocolate: It's Good for You!

When Julia Somberg eats her favorite food, she feels guilty. She knows that chocolate can have a lot of fat and sugar. But Julia says she is addicted to chocolate—once she starts eating it, she can't stop.

Julia isn't the only one who loves chocolate. It is a favorite food for people all over the world. In a survey of 16 different countries, people preferred chocolate over ice cream, cakes, and cookies. In the United States, chocolate is a $10 billion industry. For Valentine's Day, people spend over $400 million on chocolate.

The idea of *eating* chocolate didn't begin until the 19th century. Before that, people drank chocolate. The custom began in Central America, where the Aztecs drank bowls of chocolate to stay alert. When the liquid chocolate was brought to Spain in the 1500s, people thought it was medicine because it tasted bitter, like other medicines. In fact, the people who made chocolate into drinks were either druggists or doctors.

Then people discovered that mixing chocolate with sugar made a wonderful drink. King Ferdinand of Spain loved this drink so much that he put out an order: Anyone who talked about chocolate outside the court would be killed. For about 100 years, chocolate was a secret in Spain.

Finally, people found out about chocolate, and it became a popular drink in Europe. In the 1800s, a British chocolate maker discovered a way to make chocolate smooth and velvety. Then the Swiss added milk to the chocolate. Today, most Americans prefer milk chocolate, while most Europeans prefer dark chocolate.

New research shows that chocolate is actually good for us. "Chocolate has a variety of vitamins and minerals," says a researcher in France. "It has more than 300 different chemicals. One chemical works on the part of the brain that feels pleasure. People who feel good when they eat chocolate are actually healthier. Feeling pleasure is important for health and can protect against illness." "Good chocolate doesn't have much fat or sugar. You can enjoy it if you eat a little at a time!" adds Tara Berish, another chocolate lover.

Reading Skills

READING COMPREHENSION

Read the story carefully and put these events in order.

_____ Druggists and doctors made chocolate into drinks.

_1_ The Aztecs drank chocolate to stay alert.

_____ Smooth chocolate became popular in Britain.

_____ Chocolate was a secret in Spain for 100 years.

_____ Liquid chocolate was brought to Spain from Central America.

_____ Sugar was added to chocolate to make a sweet drink.

_____ Research has shown that chocolate is good for us.

_____ The Swiss added milk to the chocolate mixture.

UNDERSTAND CAUSE AND EFFECT

The word **because** *shows the cause of an action or situation.*
Match the effects in List A with the causes in List B.

List A

1. Julia feels guilty __e__

2. Julia says she can't stop eating chocolate ____

3. The Aztecs drank chocolate ____

4. People thought chocolate was a medicine ____

5. No one in Spain could talk about chocolate ____

6. Researchers say chocolate is good for us ____

7. People who eat chocolate are healthier ____

8. Good chocolate is not so fattening ____

List B

a. because it doesn't have much fat and sugar.

b. because the king put out an order.

c. because it kept them alert.

d. because it has vitamins and minerals.

e. because most chocolate has fat and sugar.

f. because feeling pleasure can protect against illness.

g. because it tasted bitter.

h. because she is addicted to it.

UNDERSTAND FACT AND OPINION

A fact is something you can see or prove. An opinion is what someone thinks or believes. Read these sentences with a partner. Decide if the information is a fact or an opinion. Write F for fact or O for opinion.

1. Chocolate is the best dessert in the world. __O__

2. Chocolate has a variety of vitamins and minerals. ____

3. Chocolate is a $10 billion industry in the United States. ____

4. Chocolate tastes better than ice cream or cookies. ____

5. You should feel guilty when you eat chocolate. ____

6. Chocolate has more than 300 different chemicals. ____

7. Milk chocolate tastes better than dark chocolate. ____

8. The Swiss were the first to add milk to chocolate. ____

Put It Together

Recycle the vocabulary from the unit. Complete the chart by putting these words into the correct categories.

	Description of Food	**Action**
1. crisp	✓	
2. roast		
3. juicy		
4. bitter		
5. bake		
6. visit		
7. enjoy		
8. fuzzy		
9. use		
10. creamy		
11. discover		
12. prepare		
13. pick		
14. fresh		
15. sweet		
16. feel		
17. protect		
18. smooth		

TALK ABOUT IT

Discuss these questions in groups.

1. What is your favorite food?
2. How often do you eat it?
3. Do you ever feel guilty when you eat this food? Why or why not?
4. Are there any foods you dislike or hate? What are they?
5. Are there any foods you don't eat because you think they are bad for your health? What are they?
6. Do you try new foods often?
7. What is your favorite dessert?
8. How often do you eat it?
9. Why do so many people love chocolate?
10. Why do so many people feel guilty when they eat chocolate?

TELL THE STORIES

A. Tell the story "Good Enough to Eat" to another student in the class. Imagine you have a job as a food stylist. Explain what you do and describe the difficult aspects of your job.

B. Tell the story "Eat Chocolate: It's Good for You!" to someone outside of the class. Explain:

1. where chocolate comes from.
2. why people feel guilty when they eat chocolate.
3. why chocolate can actually be good for your health.

WRITING OPTION

Write out a recipe for a dish you like. List the ingredients and explain how to prepare the dish.

BEYOND THE STORIES

A. Look for pictures of food in magazines or newspapers. Bring them to class. Discuss whether the pictures make you want to buy the food. Talk about how the food stylist might have made the food look good.

B. Do a survey on chocolate. Interview three people outside of your class. You can use the following questions to help you and add any others you can think of. Share your information in class.

1. Do you like chocolate?

2. How often do you eat it?

3. What kind do you like best?

4. How do you feel when you eat chocolate?

Creepy Critters

STORY 1   THE BUG OF YOUR DREAMS

STORY 2   ANIMAL MYTHS

Let's Get Ready

A. Work in groups to make lists of animals all of you dislike or fear. Then compare lists to see which creatures are most common.

B. Work in groups. Discuss each question below, then circle the letter of the correct answer.

1. Which creature can eat 600 mosquitoes an hour?

   a. the snake   b. the mouse   c. the bat

2. Which animal protects itself with a strong smell?

   a. the skunk   b. the pig   c. the beaver

3. Which creatures are sold in department stores in Japan?

   a. bugs   b. lions   c. horses

4. Which of these is a general name for insects?

   a. flies   b. bugs   c. ants

5. Which insects have a shiny black covering?

   a. spiders   b. cockroaches   c. beetles

6. Which of these animals hangs upside down?

    a. the bat   b. the parrot   c. the cat

7. Which animal is very nearsighted?

    a. the dog   b. the bear   c. the skunk

8. Which animal flies in the dark?

    a. the pigeon   b. the penguin   c. the bat

Before You Read

A. Complete the paragraph with words from the list.

hobby
interesting
enjoy
~~activity~~
coins
games
anything
relax
collecting

A hobby is an (1) ___activity___ people do in their spare time. Hobbies include handicrafts, (2) _____ things, and playing or watching various sports and (3) _____. Collecting is probably the most popular kind of (4) _____. Stamps and (5) _____ may be the most popular items to collect, but people collect almost (6) _____ you can think of— comic books, bubble gum wrappers, baseball cards, autographs, costumes, and even bugs. People of all ages (7) _____ hobbies because they can (8) _____ and have fun, while learning new and (9) _____ things.

B. Do you have any hobbies? Choose from the list below. In a group, discuss which things you like to do. You can add other things to the list.

collecting stamps	collecting rocks	gardening
collecting coins	painting	playing music
knitting	photography	making jewelry
sewing	weaving	cooking
woodworking	needlepoint	bird-watching
playing a sport	collecting shells	singing
playing checkers	playing chess	

The Bug of Your Dreams

Aki Takahashi was willing to pay $800 for his new acquisition. It was the bug of his dreams—a big black beetle. Aki is Japanese, and his hobby is one of the most popular in Japan—collecting bugs. Many people in Japan are crazy about bugs and will pay thousands of dollars for a prized specimen. Many even invest in bugs the way people invest in stocks in the stock market.

To buy his prized beetle, Aki went to the gardening and pet division at the Tokyu Department Store in Tokyo. This ritzy department store has shelves of beetles worth thousands of dollars. Although you can buy bugs for only $10, many of the bugs cost around $500. Bugs are so popular in Japan that no pet store is considered complete without a bug corner. Pet stores also carry a wide range of supplies for bugs, including food, cages, and pieces of logs in which the bugs can build their nests.

The Japanese have always been fascinated by bugs. In ancient times, rich people in Japan collected bugs and held competitions to identify the sounds bugs make. Poets have written poems and songs about the sounds of certain bugs. And it's not only collectors who have affection for bugs. Schoolchildren often raise beetles as class projects.

What do collectors look for? Size is important. A bigger beetle is worth more than a smaller one. Collectors also look for beetles that have all their legs and that don't have any scars on their legs. Also, the covering of the beetle should be shiny, like a well-polished car. Beetles are the most popular bugs for collectors, but people collect other bugs too. Of course, collectors don't like all the bugs they see. "Some bugs are repulsive," says Aki, "but the beetle is very elegant."

No one really knows how many people collect beetles. Because of the rise in cost, more and more people are breeding their own beetles. "You can buy the larvae and the supplies," says a breeder. "It's not very hard to raise beetles. Even a child can do it."

This has led to a problem for the people who sell bugs. Many have gone out of business. "In the past, people used to take out loans from the bank to pay for their bugs. Some bugs cost thousands of dol- lars. It was just like buying a house or a car," says a bug breeder named Yashiko Tanamini. "Now people raise their own beetles, so some breeders are in trouble." But another breeder isn't worried. "It's not so bad," says Hiro Atami. "You can't do this just for money. You have to really love the bugs."

Reading Skills

SCAN FOR THE DETAILS

Match the information in List A with the details in List B.

List A

1. Aki's acquisition __f__

2. Aki's hobby ____

3. a price often paid for bugs ____

4. examples of bug supplies ____

5. a competition held by rich people ____

6. class projects ____

7. characteristics collectors look for ____

8. Aki's opinion of beetles ____

9. why people are raising their own

   beetles ____

10. what's happening to the bug-raising

    industry ____

List B

a. size, legs, covering

b. cages, logs, food

c. collecting bugs

d. Some breeders have gone out of business.

e. up to $500

f. a big black beetle

g. They're very elegant.

h. Prices have increased too much.

i. identifying the sounds of different bugs

j. raising beetles

VOCABULARY IN CONTEXT

Find the underlined expressions in the story. Then use the context to help you find the words or expressions that mean the same.

1. the bug <u>of his dreams</u>
   a. of his fantasy
   b. in his nightmare

2. <u>crazy about</u> bugs
   a. worried about
   b. excited about

3. a <u>prized</u> specimen
   a. new
   b. treasured

4. this <u>ritzy</u> store
   a. expensive
   b. unusual

5. a bug <u>corner</u>
   a. room
   b. section

6. school <u>projects</u>
   a. homework
   b. sports activities

7. like a <u>well-polished</u> car
   a. shiny
   b. expensive

8. <u>breeding</u> their own beetles
   a. selling
   b. raising

9. <u>gone out of business</u>
   a. advertised their business
   b. ended their business

10. some breeders are <u>in trouble</u>
    a. in love with bugs
    b. losing money

RECYCLE THE VOCABULARY

Match the words that go together.

projects
loans
~~children~~
market
store
car
times
breeder

1. school ___children___
2. department _____
3. ancient _____
4. bug _____

5. well-polished _____
6. bank _____
7. stock _____
8. class _____

Before You Read

A. Discuss these questions in pairs.

1. What do skunks look like?
2. Is there any way to tell if a skunk is about to spray?
3. Do skunks have any value?
4. Why are many people afraid of bats?
5. Can you think of any reasons people would want bats near their homes?

B. Skim the story. Then discuss the answers to the questions in exercise A with your partner.

Animal Myths

If you ask people which animals they hate or fear the most, chances are you'll hear the following: skunks, bats, snakes, rats, and bugs. But some of these animals are gaining new respect.

The skunk, for example, is feared by most people because of its awful smell. But recently people have begun to rethink their ideas about skunks. "Skunks are very useful animals," says animal researcher Cheryl Briggs. "They catch rats and mice and beetles. They're great for pest control."

"Skunks are very fair," Cheryl explains. "They always warn you before they spray. They raise their tails and stamp their front feet. It's also good to know that you can spot a skunk before it sees you. We recognize the skunk by its white stripe. But skunks are very nearsighted and can't see more than three feet ahead. So if you pay attention to the skunk's warning signs (raising its tail and stamping its feet) and move away, you probably won't get sprayed."

Most people would not be too pleased if a skunk moved in under their house, and Cheryl has some advice on how to get rid of the creatures. First of all, skunks hate rap music, so if you play loud rap music, skunks generally will move away from your house after a few hours. Also, they love cheese, especially cheddar, so you don't have to pay an exterminator a lot of money. "Just put some cheese a few feet away from your house. When the skunk leaves to get the cheese, block the hole so it can't get back in," says Cheryl. But mostly, skunks just want to be left alone to do their work, which is pest control. "Some people who got rid of skunks now actually want them back," Cheryl adds.

Then there are bats. Many people are terrified of the black creatures that hang upside down and fly in the dark. Lately, however, bats have become more popular. The reason is that the last few summers have been unusually warm, with more mosquitoes than usual. Bats eat mosquitoes, sometimes up to 600 in an hour. "Bats are an environmentally friendly way to get rid of mosquitoes," says James Austin, an animal researcher.

In preparation for more hot summers, people are building bat houses in their basements or garages. The problem is that most people don't know what bats really like. James estimates that 40 percent of the bat houses will remain empty. "Bats like hot places, so bat houses should be a dark color to hold the heat inside. They should be 12 to 15 feet off the ground, but not in a tree where they will cool off too quickly when the sun sets."

"People like the idea of getting rid of mosquitoes without using harmful chemicals," says James. "Now, lots of people are inviting bats into their 'bat-chelor pads.'"

Reading Skills

UNDERSTAND MAIN IDEAS AND DETAILS

You can put the main ideas and details in note form to help you understand information in a story more clearly.

Complete the "Notes" chart by putting the details from the list below next to the correct main ideas. The first four details have been put in for you.

Details

- -useful in hot summers
- -play loud rap music
- ~~-have an awful smell~~
- -12 to 15 feet off the ground
- -block their holes
- -should be dark-colored

- -use cheese to get them out
- -are nearsighted
- -good for the environment
- -40% are empty
- -have a white stripe
- -eat 600 mosquitoes an hour

Notes

Main Ideas	Details
information about skunks	- have an awful smell
	-
	-
how to get rid of skunks	-
	-
	-
why bats are popular	-
	-
	-
characteristics of bat houses	-
	-
	-

Read the story and look for the answers that complete the sentences. Circle the letter of each correct answer.

1. Some animas that we fear are now
   a. getting more dangerous.
   b. getting more respect.

2. Skunks can be useful because they
   a. don't make noise.
   b. catch mice and rats.

3. Skunks warn people before they spray by
   a. raising their tails.
   b. raising their ears.

4. If you put some cheddar cheese near a skunk, you can
   a. save money by not getting an exterminator.
   b. make the skunk very sick.

5. Some people who get rid of skunks
   a. want them back.
   b. buy cats instead.

6. Due to the recent hot summers,
   a. there have been more mosquitoes lately.
   b. there have been fewer bats lately.

7. People now want bats because
   a. they are an environmentally safe way to get rid of mosquitoes.
   b. they can't afford to buy bug spray.

8. The reason many bat houses remain empty is that
   a. many people build bat houses in their garages.
   b. many people don't know where to put the bat houses.

UNDERSTAND CONNOTATIONS

Some words from the story suggest positive meanings. Other words suggest negative meanings. These meanings are called con-notations. Complete the chart.

	Positive Connotation	Negative Connotation
1. get rid of		✓
2. attract		
3. move away		
4. awful		
5. pleased		
6. hate		
7. fear		
8. useful		
9. fair		
10. popular		
11. harm		
12. prized		
13. fascinated		
14. repulsive		
15. respect		

Put It Together

Which information describes each animal? Complete the chart.

	Skunks	Bats	Beetles
1. are great for pest control	✓	✓	
2. stamp their feet			
3. are prized in Japan			
4. hate rap music			
5. sell for thousands of dollars			
6. can eat 600 mosquitoes an hour			
7. have a white stripe			
8. are nearsighted			
9. are sold in ritzy department stores			
10. have a shiny covering			
11. like hot places			
12. like cheddar cheese			
13. live in special houses			
14. live in cages			
15. are raised as school projects			

TALK ABOUT IT

1. Which animals do people hate or fear the most?

2. Why do people hate or fear these animals?

3. Which animals do you fear? Why?

4. Can these animals be useful to people? In what ways?

5. Why do some people collect these animals or keep them as pets?

6. Is there any danger in keeping unusual animals as pets? What are they?

TELL THE STORIES

A. Tell the story *"The Bug of Your Dreams"* to your teacher or to another student in the class. Explain the following:

1. the history of bug collecting in Japan

2. where people get the bugs

3. how people choose bugs

4. the costs involved with collecting bugs

B. Tell the story *"Animal Myths"* to another student in the class. Imagine that you found a skunk under your house. Explain why you don't want to get rid of it. Then explain why more people are building bat houses these days.

WRITING OPTION

Imagine that you live in a small town and are thinking of getting an exotic pet. Write to a pet shop in the city for information. Ask about equipment and food you'll need, as well as the cost of the pet. Add any other questions that you think are relevant to your choice of pet.

BEYOND THE STORIES

A. Look for a newspaper article about an animal. Bring it to class. Be prepared to explain the information in your own words.

B. Do a survey. Ask three people outside of class about the animals they dislike or fear the most. List the animals they mention. In the next class, share your information. Which animals were mentioned most frequently? Were any unusual animals mentioned?

Get Rich Quick

STORY 1   LIVING LIKE A CHICKEN

STORY 2   HAND OVER YOUR MUSHROOMS!

Let's Get Ready

A. Read this paragraph. Then close your book and write it as your teacher dictates it.

People have always tried to get rich quickly. Some people hunt for gold or diamonds or dig for oil. Other people marry for money or try to become famous. Some people even go on game shows and act silly or take part in medical experiments. Someone, somewhere, makes money from all these things.

B. Discuss these questions in groups. If you wanted to make money quickly, what would you do? Choose from the following list or add your own ideas.

1. marry a millionaire
2. act silly on a game show
3. work at a risky or dangerous job
4. hunt for gold
5. buy lottery tickets
6. try to invent something new

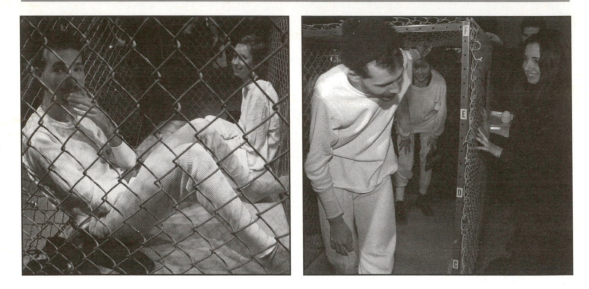

Before You Read

cages
~~billion~~
chickens
automated
plants
farms
eggs
raised

Complete the paragraph with the words below.

There are more than ten (1) _____billion_____ chickens in the world.

Some are raised on small farms to supply (2) _____ for

local markets. Most of the chickens, however, come from large

commercial (3) _____. These chickens live in wire

(4) _____ in large buildings. They eat mixes of food

made from grains and (5) _____. Chickens that are

(6) _____ for their meat live for about five to twelve

weeks. Many live on huge (7) _____ farms. Some farms

may have one million (8) _____ at a time.

Living Like a Chicken

A. How would you like an easy way to earn $2,500? All you have to do is sit around and wait for your meals. There's a catch, however. You have to stay in a chicken cage with a stranger for a whole week. There are no books or television or radio for amusement. You can't leave until the week is up. And a camera will be recording your every move.

B. Two people actually took the job. The idea came from Rob Thompson, a video artist. He wanted to make a documentary about the way animals are treated. His goal was to raise people's awareness of the living conditions of animals that are raised for food. He decided to pay $5,000 out of his own savings to two people who were willing to live like chickens for a week.

C. To Rob's surprise, quite a few people answered his advertisement. He held interviews and selected Eric, a 24-year-old restaurant worker, and Pam, a 27-year-old pharmacy technician. The plan was for them to spend seven days together in a chicken cage that was six feet long and three feet wide. A camera would record their experience, which would take place in an art gallery.

D. Pam and Eric were strangers when they met, and they worried that they wouldn't get along. But they were willing to try. They put on matching long white underwear and entered the cage.

E. The week was long and difficult. They slept on a hard wooden floor. They couldn't stand up without banging their heads. They ate vegetarian mash and drank water from a garden hose. Their only privacy was a toilet surrounded by a curtain. There were no sinks, mirrors, or toothbrushes in the cage. Their only inspiration was the two framed checks that hung on the wall outside the cage. Visitors who came into the gallery were warned, "Do not feed the humans."

F. Finally it was over, and Pam and Eric emerged from their cage. They had survived the week, and they each had a $2,500 check in their hands. When Rob Thompson opened the cage, Eric came out, changed into clean clothes, and ate a chocolate bar right away. "It's great to be able to stand up," he said. Pam just changed her clothes and left. After a week of visitors and reporters watching her, she didn't want to talk to anyone.

Reading Skills

UNDERSTAND MAIN IDEAS AND DETAILS

You can put the main ideas and details in note form to help you understand information in a story more clearly.

Complete the chart by putting details from the story in the correct places. Some details have been put in for you.

Main Ideas	Details
rules for earning $2,500	- stay in cage with stranger for a week
	-
	-
	-
Rob Thompson's idea	- make documentary
	-
people selected for experiment	- Eric, 24-year-old restaurant worker
	-
problems Pam and Eric faced	- strangers when they met
	- slept on wooden floor
	-
	-
	-
	-
how experiment ended	- Eric and Pam left with $2,500 checks.
	-
	-

SUMMARIZE THE STORY

Use the notes you just made to write a short summary of the story.
Use each main idea and the details that support it to write each
paragraph of your summary.

RECYCLE THE VOCABULARY

Match the words from the story that go together.

1. wire __f__   a. hose
2. long ____   b. checks
3. art ____   c. floor
4. framed ____   d. artist
5. vegetarian ____   e. bar
6. wooden ____   f. cage
7. video ____   g. underwear
8. living ____   h. gallery
9. garden ____   i. mash
10. chocolate ____   j. conditions

GIVE YOUR OPINION

Discuss these questions in groups.

1. Would you take part in an experiment like the one described?
2. If you would do it, how much money would you want?
3. What would be the most difficult part for you?
4. How do you think Pam and Eric felt after the experiment?
5. Do you think the experiment had value? Why or why not?

REVIEW THE VOCABULARY

Use the clues below to complete the crossword puzzle.

Across

1. drug store (paragraph C)
5. came out (paragraph F)
6. entertainment (paragraph A)
8. a place to eat (paragraph C)
11. museum (paragraph C)

Down

2. publicity (paragraph C)
3. nonfiction film (paragraph B)
4. anxious (paragraph D)
6. consciousness (paragraph B)
7. people you don't know (paragraph D)
9. hitting (paragraph E)
10. without meat (paragraph E)

Before You Read

Discuss these questions in groups.

1. What foods do people eat on Thanksgiving in the United States?

2. What special foods do people eat for other holidays that you know about?

3. What are some special foods that are hard to get?

4. Which special foods are very expensive?

5. Where do mushrooms grow?

6. What are some of the dangers of harvesting wild mushrooms?

Hand Over Your Mushrooms!

A. Every October, over 1,400 hunters hit the woods in the Pacific Northwest. They're looking for something worth millions. The hunt isn't for gold, it's for mushrooms. To some people, mushrooms are more valuable than gold.

B. The mushrooms are called "matsutake." They have a wonderful scent and are highly prized in Japan. In the same way that North Americans associate Thanksgiving with eating turkey, people in Japan associate autumn with matsutake mushrooms. They often wrap single perfect matsutake mushrooms with green leaves and give them as gifts. People use the mushrooms in soups and special dishes.

C. Matsutake mushrooms grow all over, in China, Turkey, South Korea, Bhutan, and Mexico. But the best place to find them is in the United States, in the Pacific Northwest on the border of Oregon and California. There, the mushrooms grow abundantly and the quality is excellent. They can sell for $300 a pound and have even gone up to $600 a pound.

D. The mushroom hunt is a multimillion-dollar business, and it has its risks. "There are a lot of people out in the woods, and they're all looking for the same thing. The first week in October, there were more than 1,400 pickers," says a forestry official. "The harvest can produce 1.2 million pounds of the mushrooms. That's worth about $18 million. It's no wonder there are holdups." Jack Spencer, a mushroom picker, agrees. "You have to be careful," he says. "A guy with a gun can run out of the woods and say 'hand over your mushrooms.'" But most seasons are trouble free. Hunters must buy permits, and the number of hunters in the area is restricted.

E. "The challenge is finding these matsutake mushrooms," Jack says. Hunters go out into the woods with maps and suggestions from friends. They look for places where certain trees grow together. Mushroom hunters can walk for hours and find only a few mushrooms. But then suddenly, they may hit the jackpot—a huge patch of mushrooms.

F. Wayne Denny is another hunter who is looking for the jackpot. He's an experienced mushroom picker, but he has never been to this region before. He climbs up and down hills for hours, checking his map and looking behind bushes. By noon he has only a handful of the precious matsutakes. He's worried because he has a wife and children waiting at home. He wonders how he will feed them if he doesn't find the mushrooms.

G. Then he finds it—a huge area covered with the pale mushrooms. He cleans them off and fills his bucket. "A good haul for the day," he grins. He'll make close to $200 this time. But he plans to get up really early tomorrow. He's still looking for that $1,000 patch of mushrooms. "I know it's out there," he says. "I just have to find it."

Reading Skills

READ FOR THE MAIN IDEAS

Scan the story and match the paragraphs to the main ideas.

1. popularity of matsutake mushrooms in Japan __B__

2. risks of the mushroom hunt ____

3. where matsutake mushrooms grow ____

4. Wayne's final results ____

5. descriptions of Wayne's hunt experiences ____

6. challenges of the mushroom hunt ____

SCAN FOR THE DETAILS

Match the numbers to the information.

1. 1,400 __d__
2. $300 _____
3. $600 _____
4. 1.2 million _____
5. $18 million _____
6. $200 _____
7. $1,000 _____

a. the top price per pound for matsutake mushrooms
b. the amount of Wayne's profit for the day
c. the value of the Pacific Northwest harvest
~~d.~~ the number of mushroom pickers in the Pacific Northwest
e. the amount Wayne hoped to make the second day
f. the number of pounds per harvest
g. the normal price per pound for matsutake mushrooms

IDENTIFY EXAMPLES

Read the story carefully to find examples of the following:

1. something the value of matsutake mushroom is compared to

   _____ gold _____

2. two things matsutake mushrooms are used for in Japan

   _____   _____

3. four Asian countries where matsutake mushrooms grow

   _____ _____ _____ _____

4. a risk mushroom pickers face in the woods _____

5. three kinds of information hunters use to find matsutake mushrooms _____ _____ _____

6. What Wayne is still looking for _____

Find the underlined expressions in the story. Then use the context to help you choose the expression that has the same meaning.

1. hit the woods (paragraph A)

   a. cut down the trees

   b. arrive in the forest

2. have gone up to $600 (paragraph C)

   a. have increased in price

   b. have become less expensive

3. It's no wonder. (paragraph D)

   a. It's amazing.

   b. It's not surprising.

4. to hand over your mushrooms (paragraph D)

   a. give someone your mushrooms

   b. select the best mushrooms by hand

5. hit the jackpot (paragraph E)

   a. be very successful

   b. put mushrooms in a pot

6. a handful of the precious mushrooms (paragraph F)

   a. a few

   b. a lot

7. a good haul for the day (paragraph G)

   a. good results

   b. a lot of hard work

8. to make close to $200 (paragraph G)

   a. a little less than

   b. a little more than

Put It Together

Who or what is it? Match the descriptions to the items.

1. have a wonderful scent __j__
2. a good haul for the day ____
3. things you wear under your clothes ____
4. a bad place to sleep ____
5. valuable items ____
6. something hunters need____
7. what people use mushrooms for ____
8. 6 feet long, 3 feet wide ____
9. something sweet to eat ____
10. something you earn ____
11. something that gives privacy ____
12. something used to find a place ____

a. a map
b. a chocolate bar
c. a wire cage
d. a curtain
e. soup
f. a $2,500 check
g. a hard wooden floor
h. gold and diamonds
i. a bucket of mushrooms
j. matsutake mushrooms
k. underwear
l. a permit

TALK ABOUT IT

Discuss these questions in groups.

1. What kinds of things do people do to make money quickly?
2. Which things are legal? Which things are illegal? Make two lists.
3. Would you do the things in either story to make money? Why or why not?
4. Have you ever done anything difficult or unusual to make money quickly? Describe what you did.

TELL THE STORIES

A. Tell the story "Living Like a Chicken." Imagine that you are Pam or Eric. Describe:

1. your living conditions
2. how you felt in the cage
3. the problems you had
4. your motivation for taking the job
5. how you felt when it was over

B. Tell the story "Hand Over Your Mushrooms!" to another student. Imagine that you are one of the hunters in Oregon. Describe:

1. why everyone is hunting for the mushrooms
2. how you look for the mushrooms
3. how you feel when you find a big patch of mushrooms

WRITING OPTION

Imagine that you went to see the exhibit of Pam and Eric in the chicken cage. Write a letter to a friend describing the experience. Discuss the artist's ideas and explain what you saw and how you felt.

BEYOND THE STORIES

Do a survey. Ask three people outside of class what they would do if they wanted to make money quickly. List any ideas they have. Share your ideas in class. Which ideas did you hear most often?

UNIT 9

Gone Astray

STORY 1   ELISHA, THE LOST FLAMINGO

STORY 2   DUCKS AFLOAT

Let's Get Ready

A. Work in groups to do this geography quiz. Circle the letter of the correct answer for each question.

1. What is the biggest ocean in the world?
   a. Atlantic   b. Pacific   c. Arctic

2. Which place is closest to Alaska?
   a. Hawaii   b. Japan   c. Washington State

3. When it's summer in Alaska, it's winter in
   a. Spain.   b. Chile.   c. Canada.

4. When do animals migrate to warmer climates?
   a. spring   b. winter   c. fall

5. Hawaii is located in the
   a. Pacific Ocean   b. Indian Ocean   c. Caribbean Sea

6. The Gulf Stream brings warm water to

    a. Mexico.　　　　　b. Iceland.　　　　　c. Peru.

7. Where is the state of Washington?

    a. on the Gulf Coast　b. on the East Coast　c. on the West Coast

8. Where is the Bering Sea?

    a. in Alaska　　　　b. in Washington State　c. in Maine

9. Where is Korea located?

    a. near Fiji　　　　b. near Alaska　　　　c. near Japan

10. To get to Ottawa, Canada, from Connecticut, you travel

    a. north.　　　　　b. south.　　　　　c. west.

11. In autumn, birds in the northern hemisphere migrate

    a. north.　　　　　b. east.　　　　　c. south.

12. In autumn, birds in the southern hemisphere migrate

    a. north.　　　　　b. west.　　　　　c. south.

B. Work with a partner. Look at a map of the world to check some of your answers to the quiz.

Before You Read

A. Discuss these questions in groups.

1. What is migration?
2. Which animals migrate?
3. Why do animals migrate?
4. How do animals know where to go when they migrate?
5. What can happen to animals if they lose their way?

B. Classify these words into categories. Complete the chart.

	Person	Place	Bird
1. naturalist	✔		
2. duck			
3. greenhouse			
4. bird compound			
5. flamingo			
6. caregiver			
7. wildlife expert			
8. park			
9. veterinarian			
10. swan			
11. shallow pond			
12. resident			

Elisha, the Lost Flamingo

Everyone knows that flamingos are tropical birds, so when a resident of Ottawa, Canada, spotted a pale pink flamingo one cold November day, he was sure it was made of plastic. "I saw this pink flamingo standing on one leg," he said. "I was sure someone had put up a plastic bird to fool people. Suddenly the flamingo lifted its head and looked right at me. I couldn't believe it was real!"

The bird, called Elisha, was more than 300 miles from home when she landed in Ottawa. Elisha was living in a bird compound in a small town near Connecticut when she got lost. Why was the bird flying around? "She was probably trying to migrate," says a naturalist. "A flamingo's natural instinct is to migrate to warmer weather in winter. Elisha was born in Chile. Chilean flamingos' instincts are to fly north to the Andes mountains. They can survive for some time in cold weather, but no flamingo has ever tested the extreme cold of a Canadian winter," he explains.

For the past few years, Elisha has lived in a bird compound with other birds, ducks, and swans. In summer, the birds spend their time in a shallow pond. In winter they live in a large, heated greenhouse. One day, Elisha took off and flew about 50 miles to the Connecticut River. Her caregivers tried to get her back and planned to clip her wings so she wouldn't fly away again. But every time they approached, Elisha managed to get away. "That's a smart bird," said a news reporter. "She probably knew she was about to get her wings clipped."

Back in Ottawa, wildlife experts were trying to rescue Elisha before she froze to death. But it wasn't easy. First they put up a giant mirror to attract her and placed plates of food next to her. She didn't bite. Next, they gathered together plastic flamingos, the kind that are used as lawn ornaments. They set the plastic birds up in a park nearby. "We were hoping that Elisha would like being in a group, even if it is plastic. Maybe she would fall in love or something," a rescue worker said. That didn't work either. "She's not easy to catch," said a compound worker in Connecticut. "We couldn't catch her either. She seems to like her freedom."

Finally, after a dozen rescue attempts by almost 100 volunteers, Elisha was captured. "I guess she got hungry," said a rescue worker. "We were about to give up when we saw her looking for food at the edge of the river. She couldn't find anything to eat because the water was frozen." Rescue workers broke the ice and Elisha put her head in the water to feed. When she came up they caught her in a net. Later Elisha was examined by a veterinarian and given a clean bill of health. Then she flew back to Connecticut, this time by plane.

Reading Skills

READING COMPREHENSION

Read the questions and write the answers.

1. What did the Ottawa resident think when he saw a pink flamingo in November?

   <u>He thought it was a plastic bird.</u>

2. How far is it from Connecticut to Ottawa?

   _____

3. In which direction do Chilean flamingos fly in winter?

_____

4. Why did the people in the bird compound want to clip Elisha's wings?

_____

5. What happens when the caregivers tried to capture Elisha?

_____

6. Why did wildlife experts want to capture Elisha?

_____

7. Why did wildlife experts set up plastic flamingos in the park?

_____

8. Why was Elisha so hungry?

_____

9. What did rescue workers use to capture Elisha?

_____

10. Do you think Elisha will try to escape again? Why or why not?

_____

SCAN FOR THE DETAILS

Which things are true about Elisha? Put a check mark beside the ones that apply.

1. stood on one leg ✔___

2. is made of plastic ____

3. arrived in Ottawa in November ____

4. is a tropical bird ____

5. lived in a bird compound ____

6. was born in the southern hemisphere ____

7. escaped her keepers in Connecticut ____

8. was attracted by a giant mirror ____

9. fell in love with Ottawa ____

10. had her wings clipped ____

11. was saved by rescue workers ____

12. was caught by a dozen volunteers ____

13. bit the veterinarian ____

14. flew in an airplane ____

15. went back to Chile ____

READING COMPREHENSION

Put each set of sentences in order according to the story.

1. _2_ The flamingo looked at the man.

   _1_ The flamingo stood on one leg.

2. ____ Elisha lived in Connecticut.

   ____ Elisha landed in Ottawa.

3. ____ Elisha's caregivers planned to clip her wings.

   ____ Elisha flew off to the Connecticut River.

4. ____ Wildlife experts put up a giant mirror to attract Elisha.

   ____ Wildlife experts put out plastic flamingos to attract Elisha.

5. ____ Rescue workers almost gave up because they couldn't

   catch Elisha.

   ____ Rescue workers saw Elisha looking for food.

6. _____ Rescue workers caught Elisha in a net.

_____ Elisha put her head under the water.

7. _____ The flamingo flew back to Connecticut.

_____ The flamingo was examined by a vet.

CLASSIFY THE EXAMPLES

Find examples in List B that match the general categories in List A.

List A

1. places where captive birds live

   in Connecticut __f__

2. geographic places Elisha had

   been _____

3. types of birds in the story _____

4. terms for people who tried to

   rescue Elisha _____

5. professions that deal with ani-

   mals _____

6. ways Elisha flew _____

7. parts of Elisha's body _____

List B

a. her wings, airplane
b. rescue workers, compound workers, caregivers
c. veterinarian, naturalist, wildlife expert
d. ducks, swans, flamingos
e. Connecticut, Ottawa, Chile
f. pond, greenhouse
g. wings, head, leg

DUCKS AFLOAT

Before You Read

A. Match the words to the definitions.

1. a current __b__

2. a beachcomber ____

3. the shore ____

4. to bob ____

5. an oceanographer ____

6. to drift ____

a. to move up and down quickly
b. moving water or air
c. the edge of the water
d. a person who searches the beach
e. to move slowly in the water
f. a scientist who studies the oceans

B. Discuss these questions in groups.

1. How often do you go to the ocean?

2. Which oceans have you been to?

3. What kinds of things do you find on the beach?

4. Did you ever see anything floating in the water? What was it?

Ducks Afloat

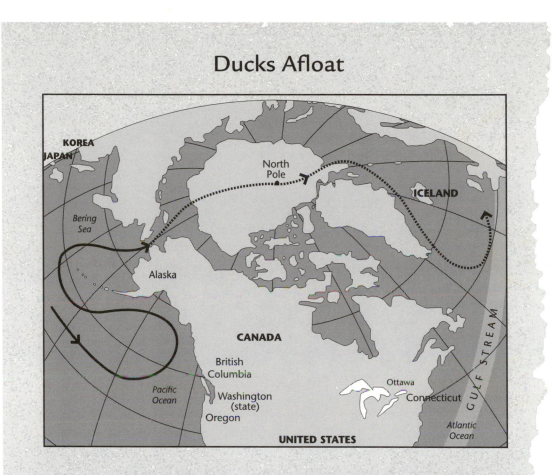

In November of 1992, people at beaches in Canada and Alaska noticed something strange: blue turtles, red beavers, green frogs, and yellow ducks came bobbing toward them. They soon found out where the strange creatures were coming from.

A ship from Hong Kong was on its way to Tacoma, Washington, when it hit a severe storm in the middle of the Pacific Ocean. During the storm, huge waves washed 12 containers overboard. Inside the containers were 29,000 plastic bath toys. One of the containers opened, and thousands of plastic bath toys spilled out and began to float across the Pacific Ocean. 10 months later, the first yellow ducks arrived on the North American shore.

Beachcombers along the shore began to find the toys and reported them to local newspapers. But the people who were most excited by the plastic toys were the oceanographers. It gave them an opportunity to study ocean currents and winds. Ordinarily, oceanographers drop bottles into the ocean to study these things. But it would be too expensive to drop 29,000 bottles into the ocean at once.

Studying the plastic ducks and frogs gave some interesting results. The first toys were picked up in Sitka, Alaska, 10 months after they were washed off the ship. Some headed back into the North Pacific, while others drifted around the Arctic Ocean and headed for the North Atlantic. Many of the toys were swept northeast by the wind and were frozen in the ice of the Bering Sea. They are expected to cross the North Pole and float on down to the British Isles.

This is similar to another unusual ocean spill. In 1990, a ship traveling to the west coast of the United States from Korea was caught in a severe storm. The waves swept 21 containers of Nike shoes into the water. Scientists estimate that about 80,000 running, jogging, and hiking shoes (40,000 pairs) hit the water at once. The shoes were for men, women, and children.

About six months later, people at beaches from Oregon to British Columbia began to find running shoes washing ashore. By the end of the year, Washington newspapers reported people finding hundreds of shoes. In Seattle, thousands of shoes floated to shore. Since the shoes were not attached, they arrived one at a time. The shoes were dirty, but after they were washed they were still in good condition. People set up exchanges to find matches for their shoes.

Oceanographers studied the information to learn more about the ocean. Some Nike shoes reached Hawaii. Others went to the Philippines and Japan. According to the scientists, some of the shoes are on a trip around the world and should end up back in Washington and Oregon.

Many pairs of running shoes, as well as plastic ducks and frogs, are still on their ocean journey. So if you go to a beach anywhere in the world, don't be surprised if you see a green plastic frog or a woman's size 7 jogging shoe bobbing toward you!

Reading Skills

Read the sentences and write T *for* true *or* F *for* false. *Correct the false information.*

1. The plastic toys were washed off the ship ~~in Alaska~~. __f__ (In the Pacific Ocean)

2. The ducks floated in the ocean for two weeks before arriving at the beach. _____

3. People who found the ducks were more excited than the oceanographers. _____

4. The floating toys made it possible to study ocean currents and winds. _____

5. All the plastic toys followed the same ocean current to their destination. _____

6. Some of the toys were crossing the Arctic Ocean to the Atlantic Ocean. _____

7. The toys and the shoes were in the water for the same reason. _____

8. The running shoes were washed overboard on a ship headed for Hawaii. _____

9. The shoes were not usable when people found them. _____

10. Some of the shoes may be carried all the way around the world. _____

SCAN FOR THE DETAILS

Write who or what did each thing.

1. <u>People at beaches in Canada and Alaska</u> noticed plastic ducks and frogs bobbing toward them.

2. _____ hit a severe storm in the Pacific Ocean.

3. _____ began to find toys along the shore.

4. _____ study ocean currents and winds.

5. _____ were picked up in Alaska 10 months after they were washed off the ship.

6. _____ are expected to cross the North Pole.

7. _____ swept 21 containers of Nike shoes into the water.

8. _____ estimate that 40,000 pairs of shoes hit the water at once.

9. _____ began to find running shoes washing ashore.

10 _____ reported people finding hundreds of shoes.

11. _____ were in good condition after they were washed.

12. _____ are still on their ocean voyage.

VOCABULARY IN CONTEXT

Circle the letter of the word or phrase that means the same as each underlined word or phrase. Reread the story if you need more context to understand the meaning.

1. Huge waves <u>washed</u> 12 containers <u>overboard</u>.
   - ⓐ moved the containers into the ocean
   - b. cleaned the containers on the ship

2. Thousands of bath toys <u>spilled out of the containers</u>.
   - a. fell out of the containers
   - b. broke inside the containers

3. Beachcombers found the toys and <u>reported them</u> to local newspapers.
   - a. brought them
   - b. talked about them

4. Some <u>headed back into</u> the North Pacific.
   - a. went away from
   - b. went toward

5. About 80,000 shoes hit the water <u>at once</u>.
   - a. at the same time
   - b. one time only

6. People began to find running shoes <u>washing ashore</u>.
   - a. washed and clean
   - b. at the shore

7. People set up exchanges to find <u>matches for their shoes</u>.
   - a. shoes of the same size
   - b. shoes they liked

8. Many shoes are still <u>on their ocean journey</u>.
   - a. traveling around the world
   - b. on ships around the world

Put It Together

Put the words into categories by completing the chart.

	Places	People	Things	Actions
1. Pacific Ocean	✓			
2. oceanographers				
3. Chile				
4. a greenhouse				
5. migrate				
6. wash ashore				
7. bath toys				
8. naturalists				
9. survive				
10. caregivers				
11. lawn ornaments				
12. containers				
13. ocean currents				
14. pick up				
15. freeze				
16. spend time				
17. hit the water				
18. scientists				
19. Bering Sea				
20. beachcombers				
21. capture				
22. veterinarians				
23. float				
24. rescue				
25. a bird compound				

TALK ABOUT IT

1. Did you ever find anything interesting at the beach? What was it?
2. What would you do if you found a running shoe or a plastic beach toy at the shore?
3. How does the study of ocean currents help people?
4. Did you ever send a message in a bottle? What did it say?
5. Why do you think people tried so hard to save Elisha?
6. Do you know any other stories about lost objects or animals?
7. Why are people interested in reading stories about animals?

TELL THE STORIES

A. Tell the story "Elisha, the Lost Flamingo." Imagine you are a news reporter following the story. First write the story in your own words. Then give your report, in your own words, to the class or to a group of students in the class.

B. Tell the story "Ducks Afloat." Imagine that you are an oceanographer on the Pacific coast of the United States and that you are describing your findings to an oceanographer in another part of the world. Explain:

1. what you found
2. how it will help you in your work
3. what you learned from studying the bath toys and the running shoes
4. how excited you were to find these things

WRITING OPTION

Imagine that you found three running shoes on the beach. They are your size but they are all for the left foot. You also found two size 12 shoes that match but are different colors and are too big for you. Write an announcement to put on a community bulletin board about the running shoes you found. Give information about how to contact you to make an exchange.

BEYOND THE STORIES

A. Does your school have a lost-and-found? If so, visit the lost-and-found to see what kinds of objects people have lost. Share your information with other students.

B. Look in the newspaper for a story about a lost object or animal. Bring the story to class. Share your information with other students.

UNIT 10

Show Biz

STORY 1   THE $100-MILLION SHOW

STORY 2   ELVIS FOREVER

Let's Get Ready

Discuss these questions in groups.

1. How often do you go to the movies?

2. What was the name of the last movie you saw?

3. What was it about?

4. Which movies are most popular now?

5. What was the best movie you ever saw?

6. Which singers or musicians are the most famous now?

7. Who is your favorite singer or musical group?

8. Which actresses and actors are famous today?

9. Who are your favorite actors and actresses?

10. What makes some singers and actors so popular?

Before You Read

A. Do a survey. Ask three students in the class about their favorite kinds of entertainment. Complete the chart. Ask: What is your favorite . . .

Name of Student			
1. movie			
2. TV show			
3. musical group			
4. actor			
5. actress			
6. female singer/musician			
7. male singer/musician			
8. TV personality			

B. Every spring the Academy of Motion Picture Arts and Sciences holds an awards ceremony in Hollywood. Discuss these questions in groups.

1. What is the ceremony called?

2. Where does it take place?

3. In what month does it take place?

4. What happens at the ceremony?

5. What are some expenses associated with this ceremony?

6. Can you think of any unusual events at the ceremonies?

7. What do you think is the most entertaining part of the ceremony?

8. Why do you think people are fascinated by Hollywood stars?

The $100-Million Show

What event lasts only three hours, employs over 10,000 people, and generates $100 million? It's the Oscars—the biggest show on earth. It is estimated that 75 million Americans watch the Oscars every March. Around the world, 98 more television stations, from Abu Dhabi to Aruba, also televise the Academy Awards.

The Oscar ceremony is the biggest, most extravagant live event on television. Although it lasts only three hours, it costs as much to produce as a Broadway play.

Thousands of people work to get the show ready. More than 600 people, including electricians, carpenters, camera technicians, and lighting experts work on building the set. Outside the theater, parking is another big expense. About 5,000 cars need to be parked, and parking all those cars can cost up to $90,000.

The Oscars are big business for people in Hollywood—from manicurists to florists to jewelry designers. A shop that specializes in makeup has its busiest time of year around Oscar day, when it takes in about $5,000 a day. Last year, the hairdresser's bill for one famous movie star was $3,000.

As the stars arrive, the focus is on their clothes. Everyone waits to see which stars have the most unusual or the most outrageous outfits. Dress designers go to extremes to get stars to choose their creations. One movie star received 56 gowns from 13 different designers. The dresses were worth from $2,000 to $20,000 each. The movie star couldn't decide which dress was the most outstanding, so her stylist encouraged designers to send more gowns for her to look at.

A famous Italian designer was concerned that the $10,000 dress he created for an Oscar-winning star would get crushed in transport. He decided to send an employee from New York to pick up the dress in Milan, bring it to the movie star for a fitting in New York, and then fly with the gown to Los Angeles.

There are other costs in producing the show as well. There is Oscar himself. Each year, 60 Oscar stat-uettes are produced, at a cost of $18,000. And there are the funny lines that the presenters use. Eleven writers work to write jokes and speeches. A 60-member orchestra plays different music for each of the 26 awards. The music alone costs $500,000. Then there is the food for the limousine drivers. While the show is on, 1,100 limousine drivers eat spicy chicken wings and green salad while they wait for their clients. Their meals cost $13,000.

After the show, the parties begin. There are more than a dozen different parties. Each party costs from $100,000 to $200,000. The glamorous stars wait for their limousines, surrounded by 10,000 beautiful flowers provided by the official Oscar florist. He flies in the most exotic flowers he can find, such as rare orchids from Hawaii, at a cost of about $750,000.

Why do the Oscars cost so much? Winning the Best Picture Award adds $139 million to a film's sales. With people so interested in celebrities, one night a year can really pay off!

Reading Skills

Complete these sentences by telling who does each thing.

1. <u>Thousands of people</u> work on getting the show ready.

2. _____ work on building the set.

3. _____ go to extremes to get a star to choose their creations.

4. _____ was concerned his dress would be crushed in transit.

5. _____ went to pick up a dress in Milan.

6. _____ write the funny lines.

7. _____ plays music for each of the awards.

8. _____ eat spicy chicken wings and green salad.

9. _____ wait for their limousines.

10. _____ flies in exotic flowers from Hawaii.

SCAN FOR THE DETAILS

Match the money spent with what it buys.

1. $18,000 __g__
2. $500,000 ____
3. $750,000 ____
4. $139 million ____
5. $100 million ____
6. $2,000–$20,000 ____
7. $90,000 ____
8. $13,000 ____
9. $5,000 ____
10. $3,000 ____

a. the cost of parking for 5,000 cars
b. what the Best Picture Award adds to a film's sales
c. one famous movie star's hairdressing bill
d. the cost of a dress for a big star
e. the cost of music for the presentation of each award
f. expenses generated around the Academy Awards
g. the cost of the 60 Oscar statuettes
h. what a makeup shop takes in each day around Oscar day
i. the cost of exotic flowers
j. the cost of meals for limousine drivers

RECYCLE THE VOCABULARY

Complete these phrases with information from the text.

1. the biggest <u>show on earth</u>

2. the most extravagant _____

3. the busiest _____

4. the most unusual or outrageous _____

5. the most outstanding _____

6. the most exotic _____

BUILD YOUR VOCABULARY

Cross out the word or words in each line that can't be used with the underlined verb.

1. You can <u>generate</u>

   money   business   ~~dresses~~   ~~employees~~   excitement

2. You can <u>televise</u>

   the Oscars   the viewers   the show   the event   the electrician

3. You can <u>produce</u>

   a play   a show   a party   a movie   a florist

4. You can <u>write</u>

   jokes   speeches   plays   scripts   presenters

Before You Read

A. Discuss these questions in groups.

1. Who was Elvis Presley?

2. What was he famous for?

3. Where did he live?

4. Can you name any of Elvis's songs?

5. Can you name any of Elvis's movies?

6. What did Elvis look like?

7. Why do you think people want to imitate him?

B. You will read about the Elvis legend. Work in a group and write five questions you think the reading may answer. For example: Why do some people believe Elvis is still alive?

1. _____

2. _____

3. _____

4. _____

5. _____

C. Skim the story to see if it talks about any of the things you thought it might.

Elvis Forever

A. Picture a room filled with people who are all dressed alike. They're wearing skin-tight black leather or white polyester jumpsuits. There are skinny people and fat ones, old ones and young ones. They all want to look like one person: Elvis Presley.

B. Every year on the anniversary of his death, thousands of people gather at Elvis's home, Graceland, in Memphis, Tennessee. They call it Elvis Week. For many people, worshipping Elvis has become almost a religion. Every year at dawn, Elvis fans gather around his grave to light candles in his honor. Some fans break down and cry. Twelve hours later, when the last candles burn out, they stagger back to their hotels and motels. Some of them go for a swim in the guitar-shaped swimming pools, or watch a 24-hour TV program of nothing but Elvis movies.

C. On the twentieth anniversary of his death, people from all over the world came to Memphis. Close to 50,000 people gathered to participate in a nine-day festival of contests and concerts. Walking down the street, you would see Italian Elvises in restaurants, German Elvises drinking "Elvis shakes," Japanese Elvises, baby Elvises, Elvises in wheelchairs, and female Elvises with stick-on sideburns. Everywhere you looked, you would see Elvises of every size and description. In fact, it was hard to find anyone who wasn't dressed like Elvis. "I'd never seen anything like it," said a cameraman covering the event.

D. Elvis is one of the most imitated people on the planet. At the festival, there were contests to find the best impersonator. A man called the Japanese Elvis did a comedy routine. The Mexican impersonator changed Elvis's song "You Ain't Nothing but a Hound Dog" to "You Ain't Nothing but a Chihuahua." "It was really silly. It wasn't like Elvis at all," said Sonia, president of an Elvis fan club. But the impersonators disagreed. "We were just worshipping Elvis in our own way," said the Liverpool Elvis.

E. What is it about Elvis Presley that makes fans continue to adore him more than 20 years after his death? Perhaps it's his rags-to-riches story, the poor boy that made it to the top. Maybe it was his love for his family. Or was it his music? "It has a wonderful blend of black and white influences plus country music," says a fan. "His music is international. I feel so good when I hear it." Elvis was also charming. "He knew how to communicate with people," says another fan. "He remembered people and made them feel special."

F. Some people think "Elvis mania" has gone too far. "He was just a human being," says a Memphis resident. "Some of the people here have no life. It's sad." But many of his fans disagree. They remember the young man who was full of life on stage, the man with the beautiful voice. Even though Elvis died many years ago, some people think his voice will live forever. A British fan says, "Last year, an Elvis album was third on the British charts!"

Reading Skills

Skim the story and decide which paragraph is mainly about the following.

1. Elvis-impersonator contests __D__

2. gatherings at Graceland ____

3. Elvis look-alikes ____

4. reasons for Elvis worship ____

5. criticisms of Elvis mania ____

SCAN FOR THE DETAILS

Who said each of these things?

1. "I'd never seen anything like it."

   <u>   a cameraman covering the event   </u>

2. "You Ain't Nothing but a Chihuahua"

   _____

3. "It wasn't like Elvis at all."

   _____

4. "We were just worshipping Elvis in our own way."

   _____

5. "He was just a human being."

   _____

6. "Last year, an Elvis album was third on the British charts."

   _____

VOCABULARY IN CONTEXT

Find words in the story that have similar meanings to the words below.

1. In paragraph A: the same ___alike___   thin ___skinny___

2. In paragraph B: sunrise _____   walk crookedly _____

3. In paragraph C: to take part _____   woman _____

4. In paragraph D: copied _____   performance _____

5. In paragraph E: love _____   mixture _____

6. In paragraph F: craze _____   music ratings _____

LANGUAGE STUDY

Match the compound adjectives with the things they describe.

1. week-long __f__

2. nine-day ____

3. guitar-shaped ____

4. 24-hour ____

5. rags-to-riches ____

6. starry-eyed ____

7. stick-on ____

8. skin-tight ____

a. swimming pool
b. fans
c. festival
d. pants
e. sideburns
f. gathering
g. story
h. TV program

Put It Together

Synonyms are words with the same meaning. Antonyms are words with opposite meanings. Look at these words or expressions from the stories. Write S for synonym or A for antonym.

1. imitate   impersonate __S__

2. creations   designs ____

3. skin-tight   loose ____

4. adore   dislike ____

5. mania   craziness ____

6. rare   unusual ____

7. break down   cry ____

8. glamorous   ordinary ____

9. celebrities   stars ____

10. visitors   residents ____

TALK ABOUT IT

Discuss these questions in groups.

1. Why do you think people are fascinated by Hollywood stars?

2. Why do people want to imitate famous people like Elvis Presley?

3. Which other celebrities do people often imitate?

4. Would you participate in a look-alike contest? Why or why not?

5. What are some disadvantages to being famous?

6. If you could meet any famous person, who would you like to meet? Explain why.

7. If you could trade places with any famous person, who would you like to be? Explain why.

TELL THE STORIES

A. Tell the story "The $100-Million Show" to some friends after class. First, ask them what they know about the Oscars. Then give them information about the number of people and the amounts of money that go into producing the show each year.

B. Tell the story "Elvis Forever" to some friends after class. First, ask them what they know about Elvis Presley. Then tell them about the festival that took place on the twentieth anniversary of his death and why people still continue to worship Elvis.

WRITING OPTION

Write a fan letter to your favorite entertainer. Tell the entertainer:

1. where and when you first heard or saw him or her

2. why you like him or her

3. how often you watch or listen to him or her

BEYOND THE STORIES

Watch a television show or movie in English. In the next class, discuss the following things in groups:

1. the name of the show

2. when you saw it

3. who was in it

4. the main idea

5. why you liked it or didn't like it

ANSWER KEY

Unit 1   What's on Our Plates?

STORY 1   RAW FOOD

Before You Read   *Page 2*

A.

2. cooked or raw	6. cooked or raw
3. cooked	7. cooked
4. cooked or raw	8. cooked
5. cooked or raw	9. cooked

Note: Other answers may be possible.

B.

2. C	3. B	4. A

Reading Skills

READING COMPREHENSION   *Page 4*

2. X healthy - sick
3. X 100°F - 120°F
4. ✓
5. X weeks - days
6. ✓
7. ✓
8. ✓
9. X nine hours - six hours
10. X sometimes - never

SCAN FOR THE DETAILS   *Page 4*

2. stove, grill, toaster, microwave
3. water
4. in the sun
5. fruits, vegetables
6. They got sick.
7. fruits, vegetables, nuts, rice, beans
8. six

2. b   3. a   4. b   5. b   6. a

STORY 2   THE FOOD THAT WIGGLES

Before You Read   *Page 6*

A.

2. T   3. F   4. T   5. F   6. F   7. T   8. T

B.

1. It's simple to make.
2. It comes in many different flavors.
3. People first started eating Jell-O in 1897.
4. In the Midwest, people add nuts, fruits, and berries to Jell-O.
5. Hospitals often serve Jell-O in cubes to people who are sick.
6. Unfortunately, nobody bought it, so Wait sold his idea to Frank Woodward for $450.
7. Now there is even a Jell-O museum in LeRoy, New York.
8. Jell-O is the most popular prepared dessert in the world.

Reading Skills

READ FOR THE MAIN IDEAS   *Page 8*

2. B   3. C   4. A   5. E

BUILD YOUR VOCABULARY   *Page 8*

Paragraph A: wiggles
Paragraph B: cubes
Paragraph C: advertised, recipes

Paragraph D: creek
Paragraph E: prepare, boxes

REVIEW THE VOCABULARY   *Page 9*

Ways to Serve Jell-O: 3, 7
Things We Add to Jell-O: 4, 8, 11
Color or Flavor: 2, 5, 6, 9, 10, 12

Put It Together

LET'S REVIEW   *Page 10*

2. People first started to eat Jell-O in 1897.
3. Juliano never eats food that is cooked.
4. Juliano's restaurant doesn't have a stove or a grill.
5. In the Midwest, people add nuts, fruits, and berries to Jell-O.
6. To make pizza, Juliano puts the crust in the sun for ten hours.

Unit 2   Where Are the Humans?

Let's Get Ready   *Page 14*

A.

2. d	6. a	10. l
3. c	7. h	11. j
4. e	8. i	12. k
5. f	9. b	

| STORY 1   WHO'S AT THE WHEEL?

Before You Read   *Page 16*

B.

2. B	4. A
3. D	5. C

Reading Skills

READING COMPREHENSION   *Page 17*

2. F (seven)	7. T
3. F (doesn't get paid)	8. T
4. T	9. F (They are fooled)
5. F (fewer)	10. F (legs)
6. F (low)	

BUILD YOUR VOCABULARY   *Page 18*

2. slow down	6. cap
3. mannequin	7. brakes
4. police department	8. break-in
5. neighborhood	

EXPLAIN WHY   *Page 19*

2. d	5. a
3. b	6. c
4. f	

STORY 2 ROBOSHOP

Before You Read *Page 20*

B.

Answers will vary.

C.

Items: magazines, toaster, sushi, food, drinks, household goods, cosmetics, watches, perfumes, pajamas, comic books, fresh flowers

Reading Skills

SCAN FOR THE INFORMATION *Page 22*

2. F (Japanese convenience store)
3. F (write the numbers on cards)
4. T
5. T
6. F (It puts the biggest things in first.)
7. F (expensive and inexpensive things)
8. T
9. F (much bigger than a vending machine)
10. T
11. T

GIVE YOUR OPINION *Page 22*

2. x   4. x   6. x   8. ✓   10. x
3. ✓   5. ✓   7. ✓   9. x
Note: Other answers may be possible.

BUILD YOUR VOCABULARY *Page 23*

2. human	6. numbers	10. big
3. open	7. store	11. employees
4. display	8. shopping baskets	12. talk
5. cards	9. toaster	

Put It Together

LET'S REVIEW *Page 24*

Person: 8, 9, 13, 15, 17, 18
Thing: 3, 4, 5, 7, 11, 14, 19, 20
Activity: 2, 6, 10, 12, 16

Unit 3 Messages of Love

Let's Get Ready   *Page 28*

A.

Person: 13, 15, 20
Message: 3, 7, 11, 17, 21
Place: 5, 14, 16, 18
Object: 9, 10, 22, 23
Feeling: 4, 6, 8, 12, 19, 24, 25

> STORY 1   SWEET TALK

Before You Read   *Page 30*

2. d	4. e	6. a
3. b	5. c	

Reading Skills

READING COMPREHENSION *Page 32*

2. b	4. b	6. a	8. b
3. b	5. b	7. b	

REVIEW THE INFORMATION *Page 33*

2. e	4. b	6. a	8. g
3. f	5. d	7. h	

REVIEW THE VOCABULARY *Page 33*

2. old	5. unhappy	8. buy
3. small	6. like	9. modern
4. big	7. stop	10. everyone

STORY 2   I SAW YOU!

Before You Read   *Page 34*

2. E	4. A
3. D	5. B

Reading Skills

SCAN FOR THE DETAILS   *Page 36*

2. Seattle
3. supermarket
4. Ellen
5. teacher, computer programmer
6. "I Saw U"
7. people in their 20s and 30s
8. Richard
9. a coffee shop
10. "I Saw U" section

READ FOR THE MAIN IDEA   *Page 36*

b

READING COMPREHENSION   *Page 37*

2. People write in looking for love.
3. "Someone saw me! I've been seen!"
4. The column is very popular.
5. "I wish I knew your name." "Where are you now?"
6. She doesn't meet many single men.
7. Richard called her.
8. They met in a coffee shop. They talked for a long time. They liked each other very much. They dated for several months. Now they are engaged. (any three)

BUILD YOUR VOCABULARY *Page 38*

Paragraph A: shy
Paragraph B: lucky
Paragraph C: advertisements, like
Paragraph D: difficult, single
Paragraph E: dated, are engaged

Put It Together

LET'S REVIEW *Page 39*

A.

Valentine's Day
dating
finding love
meeting people in the neighborhood
candy with messages
things in the newspaper
falling in love

B.

2. D	6. D	10. S
3. S	7. S	11. S
4. S	8. S	12. D
5. D	9. D	

Unit 4   What's That Sound?

Let's Get Ready   *Page 42*

2. actress, musician, opera singer
3. passenger, cabdriver, seat belt
4. restaurant, grocery store, farm
5. forehead, chin, nose
6. briefcase, hat, umbrella
7. annoyed, cheerful, relaxed
8. famous, well-known, popular,

STORY 1   MUZAK

Reading Skills

SCAN FOR THE DETAILS   *Page 46*

2. elevator music, Muzak
3. one-third
4. ten to eleven in the morning; three to four in the afternoon
5. $4 million a year
6. to make people feel less lonely
7. offices, factories
8. buy 38 percent more groceries
9. It's boring.
10. give more milk

BUILD YOUR VOCABULARY   *Page 47*

2. locations	4. recognize	6. relaxed	8. enjoy
3. songwriter	5. lonely	7. boring	

STORY 2   TALKING TAXIS

Before You Read   *Page 48*

B.

2. c   3. c   4. b

C.

1. Many people think New York is a noisy city.
2. The average noise level in New York is 72.5 decibels.
3. There are more than 12,000 cabs in New York.
4. In an accident, people who don't wear seatbelts . . .
   can bruise their foreheads or break their noses or chins.

Reading Skills

UNDERSTAND THE DETAILS   *Page 50*

2. 65 decibels	6. 12,000
3. 11,000	7. 72.5 decibels
4. 45 years old	8. 12
5. $100	9. 15,000

2. you get into a taxi.
3. they don't wear seat belts.
4. they hear the same voices sixty times a day.
5. they get fined $100.
6. they think it's too much noise.
7. they put on their seat belts more often.
8. hear a cheerful voice when she gets into a cab.

BUILD YOUR VOCABULARY *Page 52*

2. i	6. h	10. k
3. b	7. l	11. f
4. c	8. e	12. d
5. a	9. j	

Put It Together

LET'S REVIEW *Page 53*

2. A company in Seattle makes Muzak for 150,000 locations.
3. Some famous songwriters are happy when their songs are used.
4. Taxi drivers hear the same messages 60 times a day.
5. Every year, there are 15,000 accidents in taxis.
6. Voices in taxis often belong to famous people.

Unit 5   Working Up High

Let's Get Ready   *Page 57*

C.

Answers will vary.

Reading Skills

READ FOR THE INFORMATION   *Page 60*

2. a friend asked him for help painting a flagpole.
3. he bought the equipment he needed to paint more.
4. he has a unique business.
5. paint flagpoles.
6. the weather gets cold.
7. he has to climb up really high.
8. some poles are old or rusty.
9. the wind bent it over and he landed in a football field.
10. he was bruised and sore.

SCAN FOR THE INFORMATION   *Page 61*

2. 44 years old
3. colleges, schools, communities, post offices
4. 150 to 200
5. seven or eight
6. the tallest pole he ever painted
7. the pole in Kansas

BUILD YOUR VOCABULARY   *Page 62*

Paragraph A: narrow
Paragraph B: started, equipment, unique
Paragraph C: travels, gets
Paragraph D: hardest, climb, cracked
Paragraph E: tallest, bruised

CLASSIFY THE EXAMPLES   *Page 63*

2. d	4. a	6. f
3. e	5. b	7. g

STORY 2   FLYING THE SKIES

Before You Read   *Page 64*

B.

2. T	7. T
3. T	8. F (very noisy)
4. T	9. F (It was expensive.)
5. T	10. T
6. T	

Reading Skills

UNDERSTAND THE DETAILS   *Page 66*

2. ~~everyone~~ - only the rich and adventurous
3. ~~very smooth~~ - shook
4. ~~water~~ - mud
5. ~~quiet~~ - noisy
6. ~~women~~ - men
7. ~~green suits~~ - nurses' uniforms
8. ~~passengers~~ - flight attendants
9. ~~laugh~~ - smile
10. ~~divorce~~ - marry

REVIEW THE VOCABULARY   *Page 67*

2. night	4. cup	6. mud
3. passengers	5. meals	7. tea

READING COMPREHENSION   PAGE 68

In the 1920s: 4, 5, 6, 10, 12
In the 1930s: 3, 7, 8, 11
Now: 2, 9

BUILD YOUR VOCABULARY   *Page 69*

Paragraph B: cushions, cutlery
Paragraph C: landed, mud, yell
Paragraph D: luggage, block
Paragraph E: caps, dust
Paragraph F: gradually, attractive
Paragraph G: uniforms

Put It Together

Across	Down
5. flight attendants	2. safe
7. air	3. break
9. uniforms	4. stewardesses
11. services	6. noisy
13. modern	8. Airplanes
14. tallest	10. high
	12. sick

Unit 6   What Makes You Hungry?

Let's Get Ready   *Page 75*

B.

2. dark chocolate	8. sweet
3. guilt	9. stale
4. asleep	10. solid
5. full	11. smooth
6. easy	12. thin
7. illness	

STORY 1   GOOD ENOUGH TO EAT

Before You Read   *Page 76*

2. b	5. a
3. e	6. d
4. f	

Reading Skills

SKIM FOR THE INFORMATION   *Page 78*

2. F (because he uses techniques to make it look good)
3. F (to make them look crisp)
4. F (Grocers hate them.)
5. T
6. F (It's a challenge.)

SCAN FOR THE DETAILS   *Page 78*

2. ice cream
3. food stylist
4. 30 million
5. instant mashed potatoes
6. paintbrush, glue, pins
7. 117
8. ten
9. peaches
10. foot spray

USE THE CONTEXT TO FIND THE MEANING   *Page 79*

2. Not everything is the way it looks.
3. make advertiser's products look good
4. roasted garlic heads
5. cakes
6. peaches

RECYCLE THE VOCABULARY   *Page 79*

2. c   6. d
3. b   7. f
4. g   8. a
5. h

STORY 2   EAT CHOCOLATE: IT'S GOOD FOR YOU!

Before You Read   *Page 80*

2. F (Valentine's Day)
3. T
4. T
5. F (prefer milk chocolate)
6. T
7. F (feel pleasure)
8. T

Reading Skills

READING COMPREHENSION   *Page 82*

3, 1, 6, 5, 2, 4, 8, 7

UNDERSTAND CAUSE AND EFFECT   *Page 83*

2. h   6. d
3. c   7. f
4. g   8. a
5. b

UNDERSTAND FACT AND OPINION   *Page 84*

2. F   6. F
3. F   7. O
4. O   8. F
5. O

Put It Together

LET'S REVIEW   *Page 85*

Descriptions of Food: 3, 4, 8, 10, 14, 15, 18
Actions: 2, 5, 6, 7, 9, 11, 12, 13, 16, 17

Unit 7   Creepy Critters

Let's Get Ready   *Page 88*

B.

2. a
3. a
4. b
5. c

6. a
7. c
8. c

STORY 1   THE BUG OF YOUR DREAMS

Before You Read   *Page 90*

A.

2. collecting
3. games
4. hobby
5. coins

6. anything
7. enjoy
8. relax
9. interesting

Reading Skills

SCAN FOR THE DETAILS   *Page 92*

2. c
3. e
4. b

5. i
6. j
7. a

8. g
9. h
10. d

VOCABULARY IN CONTEXT   *Page 93*

2. b
3. b
4. a

5. b
6. a
7. a

8. b
9. b
10. b

RECYCLE THE VOCABULARY   *Page 93*

2. store
3. times
4. breeder
5. car

6. loans
7. market
8. projects

Reading Skills

UNDERSTAND MAIN IDEAS AND DETAILS   *Page 96*

information about skunks	- have an awful smell
	- are nearsighted
	- have a white stripe
how to get rid of skunks	- play loud rap music
	- block their holes
	- use cheese to get them out
why bats are popular	- useful in hot summers
	- good for the environment
	- eat 600 mosquitoes an hour
characteristics of bat houses	- 12 to 15 feet off the ground
	- should be dark-colored
	- 40% are empty

READING COMPREHENSION   *Page 98*

2. b   6. a
3. a   7. a
4. a   8. b
5. a

UNDERSTAND CONNOTATIONS   *Page 99*

Positive Connotation: 2, 5, 8, 9, 10, 12, 13, 15
Negative Connotation: 3, 4, 6, 7, 11, 14

Put It Together

LET'S REVIEW   PAGE 100

Skunks: 2, 4, 7, 8, 12
Bats: 6, 11, 13
Beetles: 3, 5, 9, 10, 14, 15

Unit 8   Get Rich Quick

STORY 1   LIVING LIKE A CHICKEN

Before You Read   *Page 104*

2. eggs
3. farms
4. cages
5. plants
6. raised
7. automated
8. chickens

Reading Skills

UNDERSTAND MAIN IDEAS AND DETAILS   *Page 106*

rules for earning $2,500	- stay in cage with stranger for a week
	- no books, TV, or radio
	- can't leave the cage
	- camera records every move
Rob Thompson's idea	- make documentary
	- raises awareness of animal living conditions
people selected for experiment	- Eric, 24-year-old restaurant worker
	- Pam, 27-year-old pharmacy technician
problems Pam and Eric faced	- strangers when they met
	- slept on wooden floor
	- ate vegetarian mash
	- drank from a garden hose
	- no privacy
	- no sinks, mirrors, toothbrushes
how experiment ended	- Eric and Pam left with $2,500 checks
	- Eric ate chocolate bar, changed clothes
	- Pam changed clothes and left

RECYCLE THE VOCABULARY   *Page 107*

2. g	5. i	8. j
3. h	6. c	9. a
4. b	7. d	10. e

REVIEW THE VOCABULARY   *Page 108*

Across
1. pharmacy
5. emerged
6. amusement
8. restaurant
11. art gallery

Down
2. advertisement
3. documentary
4. worried
6. awareness
7. strangers
9. banging
10. vegetarian

STORY 2   HAND OVER YOUR MUSHROOMS!

Reading Skills

READ FOR THE MAIN IDEAS   *Page 112*

2. D	4. G	6. E
3. C	5. F	

SCAN FOR THE DETAILS   *Page 113*

2. g	4. f	6. b
3. a	5. c	7. e

IDENTIFY EXAMPLES   *Page 113*

2. soups, special dishes
3. China, Turkey, South Korea, Bhutan
4. holdups
5. maps, advice from friends, places where certain trees grow together
6. a $1,000 patch of mushrooms

VOCABULARY IN CONTEXT   *Page 114*

2. a	6. a
3. b	7. a
4. a	8. a
5. a	

Put It Together

LET'S REVIEW   *Page 115*

2. i	6. l	10. f
3. k	7. e	11. d
4. g	8. c	12. a
5. h	9. b	

Unit 9   Gone Astray

Let's Get Ready   *Page 118*

2. c	6. b	10. a
3. b	7. c	11. c
4. c	8. a	12. a
5. a	9. c	

STORY 1   ELISHA, THE LOST FLAMINGO

Before You Read   *Page 120*

B.

Person: 6, 7, 9, 12
Place: 3, 4, 8, 11
Bird: 2, 5, 10

Reading Skills

READING COMPREHENSION   *Page 122*

2. 300 miles
3. north
4. so she wouldn't fly away again
5. She managed to get away.
6. They didn't want her to freeze to death.
7. They were hoping Elisha would like being in a group.
8. She couldn't find food because the river was frozen.
9. a net

SCAN FOR THE DETAILS   *Page 123*

3, 4, 5, 6, 7, 11, 14

READING COMPREHENSION *Page 124*

2. 1, 2   4. 1, 2   6. 2, 1
3. 2, 1   5. 1, 2   7. 2, 1

CLASSIFY THE EXAMPLES *Page 125*

2. e   4. b   6. a
3. d   5. c   7. g

STORY 2   DUCKS AFLOAT

Before You Read   *Page 126*

A.

2. d   4. a   6. e
3. c   5. f

Reading Skills

READING COMPREHENSION *Page 129*

2. F (ten months)
3. F (The oceanographers were more excited.)
4. T
5. F (different currents)
6. T
7. T
8. F (for the west coast)
9. F (They were dirty but in good condition.)
10. T

SCAN FOR THE DETAILS *Page 130*

2. A ship from Hong Kong
3. Beachcombers
4. Oceanographers
5. The first toys (yellow ducks)
6. Many of the toys
7. The waves
8. Scientists
9. People on the beaches (of Oregon and British Columbia)
10. Washington newspapers
11. The shoes
12. Running shoes and plastic ducks and frogs

2. a	6. b
3. b	7. a
4. b	8. a
5. a	

Put It Together

LET'S REVIEW *Page 132*

Places: 3, 4, 19, 25
People: 2, 8, 10, 18, 20, 22
Things: 7, 11, 12, 13
Actions: 5, 6, 9, 14, 15, 16, 17, 21, 23, 24

Unit 10   Show Biz

STORY 1   THE $100-MILLION SHOW

Reading Skills

READING COMPREHENSION *Page 139*

2. More than 600 people
3. Dress designers
4. A famous Italian designer
5. An employee from New York
6. Eleven writers
7. A 60-member orchestra
8. The limousine drivers
9. The glamorous stars
10. The official Oscar florist

SCAN FOR THE DETAILS *Page 140*

2. e	5. f	8. j
3. i	6. d	9. h
4. b	7. a	10. c

RECYCLE THE VOCABULARY   *Page 141*

2. live event on television
3. time of year
4. outfits

5. dress
6. flowers

BUILD YOUR VOCABULARY   *Page 141*

2. the viewers, the electrician
3. a party, a florist
4. presenters

STORY 2   ELVIS FOREVER

Reading Skills

READ FOR THE MAIN IDEAS   *Page 145*

2. B   3. C   4. E   5. F

SCAN FOR THE DETAILS   *Page 145*

2. a Mexican Elvis impersonator
3. Sonia, president of an Elvis fan club
4. the Liverpool Elvis
5. a Memphis resident
6. a British fan

VOCABULARY IN CONTEXT   *Page 146*

2. dawn, stagger
3. participate, female
4. imitated, routine

5. adore, blend
6. mania, charts

LANGUAGE STUDY   *Page 146*

2. c   4. h   6. b   8. d
3. a   5. g   7. e

Put It Together

LET'S REVIEW   *Page 147*

2. S   5. S   8. A
3. A   6. S   9. S
4. A   7. S   10. A

ACKNOWLEDGMENTS

"Raw Food" used by permission of Juliano and Raw Restaurant; "Who's at the Wheel?" adapted from "A Super Police Officer, But Still a Real Dummy," by Michael Janofsky, the *New York Times;* "RoboShop" as adapted from "Store Runs by Robots" by Kevin Sullivan, the *Washington Post;* "Sweet Talk" used by permission of Walter J. Marshall and the New England Confectionary Company; "I Saw U" as adapted from "Say It with Sightings" by Carey Goldberg, the *New York Times;* "Talking Taxis" adapted from "You Get In, Then It's Yada, Yada, Yada" by Neil MacFarquhar, the *New York Times;* "At the Top of the World" used by permission of Tom Freeman; "Flying the Skis" as adapted from *The Way We Are* by Margaret Visser (Toronto: HarperCollins, 1994); "Good Enough to Eat" reprinted by permission of Brett Kurzweil; "Eat Chocolate: It's Good for You!" used by permission of Julia Somberg; "Living Like a Chicken" used by permission of Robert Thompson.